The Bible Meets You
Where You Are . . .

The Bible Meets You Where You Are . . .

Personal and Group Studies
For Using the Bible in Everyday Life

DON POSTERSKI

WORD BOOKS
PUBLISHER
WACO,TEXAS

THE BIBLE MEETS YOU WHERE YOU ARE . . .

ISBN 0-8499-2857-5
Library of Congress catalog card number: 78-65803
Printed in the United States of America

Contents

Mindset of the Studies

I was weaving through traffic on my way to the university campus and listening to a student reflect on his life. He was a struggling Christian. He was also a troubled person. I remarked about God's understanding and referred to the study on depression which I was developing. The one-sided conversation which followed tumbled out this way:

"Last summer almost brought the curtain down for me. I suddenly faced myself. Here I was in my thirties. I didn't have anything significant and didn't know what I wanted. I was feeling worthless and useless. I hit the skids. Depression . . . I can tell you about depression! And if you are going to spread that gospel stuff, it better touch people where they are, or forget it!"

This conversation brought to mind an observation which I had made before but which continues to amaze me: *The Scriptures reach out and touch people where they are.* The following studies are structured to reach out and touch—to reach from God's Word and touch people in their real life situations.

In developing these studies, I continually strove for a balance between objective biblical truth and subjective personal experience. Therefore, some questions and group stimulators are cold and analytical while others are intensely intimate and personal. Some call for clear-mind responses while others call for gut-level reactions. The resulting pattern is a repeated movement from the rational to the relational and from the theoretical toward the practical.

The studies are designed for both small group and individual investigation. The group process will enhance the value of the study sessions. We do learn from each other. We are more insightful together than we are alone. Guided discussion often acts as a catalyst for our personal thinking and changes in our behavior. The studies are also suitable for those wanting to go solo. The personal approach will be adequately guided by specific and intensive questions. Numerous teaching statements will protect the individual from futile detours and dead-end journeys. The studies will serve those persons who utilize guides during their private quiet time.

To take the Scriptures seriously is to live dangerously. God's Word is an instruction book for those who are marching to the drumbeat of Jesus Christ in a world that hears other music. Bible study and reflection that grind to a halt before ideas are lived out and truth is practiced result in spiritual constipation and eventual hypocrisy. Understanding without obedience lacks integrity and makes the gospel bad news in the eyes of a secular society.

My aspirations will be reached if the studies are a medium to clearly communicate God's good news and give a sound basis for spiritual health and wholeness that can be tangibly and confidently expressed in our world.

1. The Bible Meets You Where You Are

Asking Troublesome Questions . . .

Does God Exist?

What Is God Like?

What If I Believe in God?

How Should God's People Behave?

Does God Exist?

Discussions with honest atheists in our society are a rare treat. They are rare because there are so few clear-thinking people who have concluded that God does not exist. The encounters are a treat because they offer the opportunity for stimulating interaction. When the occasion for such an exchange arises, as a person who believes that God in the Christian sense does exist, I delight in challenging the atheist with statements like—"The one thing I admire about you is your faith. Frankly, you have more faith than I do. From my view of the evidence, it takes more faith to conclude that God does not exist than it does to accept the claim of his existence."

Acceptance of the fact that God's existence cannot be proven in a scientific or test tube fashion is a struggle for some people. These same people would do well to realize that a denial of the reality of God is a statement of incredible faith and ungrounded reason.

1. Discuss the difficulties involved in "proving" some things that are widely accepted as facts. For example—prove that pain exists, prove that your mother loves you, and prove that God does exist.

2. Divide your group in half and prepare for a debate. In controlled debate fashion, respond to the claim: "Be it resolved that God does not exist."

Realizing that "facts do not cease to exist because they are

11

ignored," the outcome of the debate does not have to resolve
the issue. Let's gather some more evidence from the biblical
perspective.

3. Note: Genesis 1: 1 (RSV) "In the beginning God created
the heavens and the earth."

What position does the Bible take regarding the existence of God?

Why do you think the Scriptures simply assume and
preclude the existence of God?

Romans 1: 18–23 (RSV)

For the wrath of God is revealed from heaven against all un-
godliness and wickedness of men who by their wickedness
suppress the truth. [19] For what can be known about God is
plain to them, because God has shown it to them. [20] Ever since
the creation of the world his invisible nature, namely, his eternal power and deity, has been clearly perceived in the things
that have been made. So they are without excuse; [21] for al-
though they knew God they did not honor him as God or give
thanks to him, but they became futile in their thinking and
their senseless minds were darkened. [22] Claiming to be wise,
they became fools, [23] and exchanged the glory of the immortal
God for images resembling mortal man or birds or animals or
reptiles.

1. How does God reveal himself to people?

2. What behavior in people does God react against?

3. What does this tell us about God?

4. What are the results of ignoring God?

5. Look around your society—what are some of the consequences of disregarding God?

6. Look at yourself—what have been the results when you
have ignored God?

Does God exist or not? We must face the dilemma and
choose. The stakes are too high to ignore the issue. We must
take sides. We cannot afford to opt out. We must push our
choice to accept God's existence on to the practical consequences of that belief. We must move beyond debate and
theory to life and behavior.
    If God does not exist,
        *What are the practical consequences for me and our
        world?*

    If God does exist,
        *What are the practical consequences for me and our
        world?*

What Is God Like?

We have hunches about what God is like. In our creative and
reflective moments, we sometimes take snapshots of our Creator.

We see God as the sun—a source of energy, strong, warm, and life-giving.

We hear God as music—a melody in his creation, singing, chanting, and sometimes in the sound of silence.

We feel God as the wind—making his presence known, but not knowing from where he came or where he has gone.

1. Complete the statement "To me, God is like. . . ."

2. Take a quick journey through the four chapters in the book of Jonah. What are some of the things God does in the Jonah event? Based on God's actions, behavior, and accomplishments, what can we conclude about him?

	What did God Do?	*Conclusions about God*
Chapter 1		
Chapter 2		
Chapter 3		
Chapter 4		

Get ready for a startling revelation—JESUS IS GOD! Jesus is God in brilliant color. Jesus is a series of still life portraits describing God. Jesus is a full-length feature film demonstrating who God is and what he is like. As a result, if you are still having difficulty focusing on what God is like—take a careful look at Jesus. We see God in action during one of Jesus' visits to

Jerusalem. The account of what happened is given in John 5: 2–11.

John 5: 2–11 (rsv)

Now there is in Jerusalem by the Sheep Gate, a pool, in Hebrew called Bethzatha, which has five porticoes. [3] In these lay a multitude of invalids, blind, lame, paralyzed. [5] One man was there, who had been ill for thirty-eight years. [6] When Jesus saw him and knew that he had been lying there a long time, he said to him, "Do you want to be healed?" [7] The sick man answered him, "Sir, I have no man to put me into the pool when the water is troubled, and while I am going another steps down before me." [8] Jesus said to him, "Rise, take up your pallet, and walk." [9] And at once the man was healed, and he took up his pallet and walked.

Now that day was the sabbath. [10] So the Jews said to the man who was cured, "It is the sabbath, it is not lawful for you to carry your pallet." [11] But he answered them, "The man who healed me said to me, 'Take up your pallet, and walk.'"

1. Where else might Jesus have gone to avoid the sick and needy?

2. How did Jesus respond to the extremely ill man? What did Jesus do?

3. What does the question—"Do you want to be healed?" reveal about what God is like?

4. In what areas of your life would you welcome God's touch of healing and health?

5. Do you find yourself attracted toward Jesus? Is he the kind of person you would like for a friend? What are your reasons?

6. Reflect on both encounters—God with Jonah and Jesus with the sick man—then complete the statement: "What I appreciate more about God is . . ."

What If I Believe in God?

Some people carry a "God grudge" around on their shoulders. In their confusion about who God is and what he is like, they keep their distance and reject a relationship with their Creator.

Other people respond to God with a simple "I believe" or read a printed prayer, hoping that will be enough for a free pass into heaven. They would be better off withholding their token response.

The thoughtful person who moves toward God and chooses His ways, knows there are some strings attached. He understands something about the cost of real belief in God. He knows that God is wanting to reconstruct his life—to regroove his thinking, to alter his attitudes, to shake up his value system, and to adjust his lifestyle. The informed seeker also knows that the God who designed him is trustworthy, concerned about his best interests, and deserving of his confidence and obedience.

John 3: 16–18 and 1 John 3: 16–18 communicate part of both the consequences and cost of believing in God.

John 3: 16–18 (rsv)

For God so loved the world that he gave his only Son, that whoever believes in him should not perish but have eternal life. ¹⁷ For God sent the Son into the world, not to condemn the world, but that the world might be saved through him. ¹⁸ He who believes in him is not condemned; he who does not believe is condemned already, because he has not believed in the name of the only Son of God.

1. When God the Father sent Jesus, his Son, into the world, God's action was a demonstration of his initiative. What motivated God to send Jesus to planet earth? Why was Jesus sent?

2. What does it mean "to believe" in Jesus?

3. From the text, what are the consequences of believing in Jesus?

4. List at least five examples of condemnation in our society.

5. What does condemnation produce?

6. What does belief in Jesus produce? (Choose as many of the following phrases as you think appropriate.)
____Church goers and budget dollars
____Righteous snobs
____Servants and lovers

____Moral minus signs
____Anti-laughter lobbyists
Other__

1 John 3: 16–18 (rsv)

By this we know love, that he laid down his life for us; and
we ought to lay down our lives for the brethren. But if any
one has the world's goods and sees his brother in need, yet
closes his heart against him, how does God's love abide in him?
Little children, let us not love in word or speech but in deed
and in truth.

1. Who are Jesus' followers instructed to love?

2. How are Jesus' followers instructed to love? Observe
both the positive and negative expressions.

3. What is your honest reaction to the radical and costly demands of love?

4. What needs do you see:
   Down your block?

   In your inner city?

   On your campus?

   In your world?

5. Whom do you know personally or through other information sources who has these specific needs? List names and
situations.

6. What does God want you to *do* about the needs and the
individual people involved?

How Should God's People Behave?

"Behave yourself! Try to act like a civil human being!" Parents
have devised an unlimited number of "behave-yourself"
declarations that call their children to act properly.

In a similar sense, God exclaims to his children: "Behave
yourself! Try to act like a member of my family."

How should God's people behave? The issue of Christian
behavior has been a controversial matter within the family
of God. Some followers of Jesus are ready to write a thick rule
book in response to the question. Other Christian believers
are content to live with the single guideline of "love God and
do as you please."

Rather than debating the issue from opposite poles of opin-
ion, the better approach is for us to search the Scriptures for
God's directives regarding how he wants his people to behave.
A solid launching pad for learning to fly according to God's
behavior flight plan is found in Romans 12: 3–21.

Romans 12: 3–21 (TEV)

And because of God's gracious gift to me, I say to all of
you: Do not think of yourselves more highly than you should.
Instead, be modest in your thinking, and judge yourself according to the amount of faith that God has given you. [4]We
have many parts in the one body, and all these parts have
different functions. [5]In the same way, though we are many,
we are one body in union with Christ and we are all joined
to each other as different parts of one body. [6]So we are to use
our different gifts in accordance with the grace that God has
given us. If our gift is to speak God's message, we should do
it according to the faith that we have; [7]if it is to serve, we
should serve; if it is to teach, we should teach; [8]if it is to encourage others, we should do so. Whoever shares with others,
should do it generously; whoever has authority, should work
hard; whoever shows kindness to others, should do it cheer-
fully.

[9]Love must be completely sincere. Hate what is evil, hold
on to what is good. [10]Love one another warmly as Christian
brothers, and be eager to show respect for one another. [11]Work
hard and do not be lazy. Serve the Lord with a heart full of
devotion. [12]Let your hope keep you joyful, be patient in your
troubles, and pray at all times. [13]Share your belongings with
your needy fellow Christians, and open your homes to stran-
gers.

[14]Ask God to bless those who persecute you—yes, ask him
to bless, not to curse. [15]Be happy with those who are happy,
weep with those who weep. [16]Have the same concern for
everyone. Do not be proud, but accept humble duties. Do not
think of yourselves as wise.

[17]If someone has done you wrong, do not pay him back
with evil. Try to do what all men consider to be good. [18]Do
everything possible on your part to live in peace with every-
body. [19]Never take revenge, my friends, but instead let God's
anger do it. For the scripture says, "I will take revenge, I will
pay back, says the Lord." [20]Instead, as the scripture says: "If
your enemy is hungry, feed him; if he is thirsty, give him to

drink; for by doing this you will make him burn with shame."
[21] Do not let evil defeat you; instead, conquer evil with good.

1. In verse 3—what is the negative command? What is the positive command?

What are the implications of thinking too highly of oneself? or in the other extreme, depreciating one's worth and abilities?

2. The Scriptures use the complexity of the physical body as an analogy to describe the diversity of the community of believers who are united in Christ. A part of the diversity is demonstrated through different gifts of the Spirit being given by God to individual members of the body of Christ. Identify the gifts listed and give tangible examples of how a specific gift can be expressed.

THE GIFTS OF THE SPIRIT	HOW THE GIFTS ARE EXPRESSED
1.	
2.	
3.	
4.	
5.	
6.	
7.	

3. From the information in verses 9 through 21, make two lists—one including the ways Christians are *told to behave* and another listing the kinds of behavior Christians are *told to avoid*.

TO DO	TO AVOID

4. If people follow the above instructions, what will be the results?

5. Are you attracted to or turned off by the above way of life? Why?

6. Has the above information altered your view of how a Christian is to behave? Why or why not?

7. Paraphrase verses 9–21. Include your personal circumstances, the names of your friends, details about your family, and thoughts about your school, city, town or rural area.

For example: "God, I don't want to fake a Christian life anymore. I want to be real. Help me to develop a distaste for what is wrong and be attracted to what is right. Help me to really care about the interests of my wife, Beth, and the guys I work with. Free me so I can genuinely compliment George and Jim on the job. . . ."

2. The Bible Meets You Where You Are

Resolving Relationships . . .

> *Our Relationship with God*
>
> *Our Relationship with Ourselves*
>
> *Our Relationship with the People in Our Lives*
>
> *Our Relationship with Our World*

Our Relationship with God

The crowd was buzzing. Jesus had just out-maneuvered a shrewd priest who had fabricated a trick question. He was ready to leave but questions kept knifing through the air. Just as Jesus was turning to move on, a lawyer spoke up and asked: "Of all the commandments about which you speak—which is the most important?"

Jesus thought for a brief moment and then replied with confidence: "First, you must love God with your whole self, you are also to love yourself, and you are to love the people in your life."

The conclusion is clear. God's pattern for his people is for them "to love." But how do we love God? What is this God we are to love really like? Is he lovable? What does he require?

Acknowledging that our relationship with God is affected by our concept of him, from your personal vantage point, what is God like? How do you view him? Identify one of the following descriptions. Share the reason for your choice with your fellow group members.

a) Righteous Ruler—

b) Empathetic Psychiatrist—

c) Roving Policeman—

d) Loving Father—

e) Harsh Judge—

f) Other__

John 15: 9–14 (rsv)

As the Father has loved me, so have I loved you; abide in my love. [10] If you keep my commandments, you will abide in my love, just as I have kept my Father's commandments and abide in his love. [11] These things I have spoken to you, that my joy may be in you, and that your joy may be full.

[12] This is my commandment, that you love one another as I have loved you. [13] Greater love has no man than this, that a man lay down his life for his friends. [14] You are my friends if you do what I command you.

1. Isolate the commands God gives to his people in this passage.

2. Jesus links a loving response to God with obeying his commandments. From your memory and other biblical passages, compile a list of additional commandments God has called his people to follow. (Note: Exod. 20: 1–20, Micah 6: 8, Rom. 12: 1–21, Gal. 5: 19–23, Eph. 4: 1–3, Col. 3: 5–17, 1 Tim. 6: 11.)

3. From the list of additional commandments, which three would you like to delete? Why?

4. We express our love of God by obeying his commandments but there are times when we find it difficult to obey. Why do we often struggle to obey God?

5. Jesus not only links love and obedience together, but he also contends that our obeying will lead to a joyful life. Remembering who God is and reflecting on what he is like, on what basis can we conclude that joy will be the result of our obedience?

6. One of God's commandments is to demonstrate our love for him by loving the people around us. Recognizing that Christian love is more a choice to obey than it is a feeling to be expressed:
     Why do we sometimes fail to love each other?

     What are some of the consequences for those who learn to love each other?

7. From the people who are a part of your life, choose one person you believe God would have you love for him in this coming week. Creatively think how you can communicate your love to that person in a specific way. Share your plan of action. Now do it!

Our Relationship with Ourselves

In recent months a heavyweight gal lumbered into my office, slumped clumsily into one of the larger and more sturdy chairs, hung her head to avoid eye contact, and in despair blurted out, "I don't like me!" In a moment of honesty, I wanted to come back with, "I don't blame you!"

"Olive Overweight" eventually revealed more serious problems than how high she tipped the scales. Her self-concept was woeful. She was convinced of being both worthless and useless. Olive rated herself on the minus side in her personal value system. She was hurting and broken inside.

Olive desperately needed a new view of herself. She needed God's view of both her worth and dignity as a person made in the image of her Creator. Olive is not alone. Our self-worth needs to be affirmed too. Let's discover more of the meaning of a right relationship with ourselves. . . .

Genesis 1: 26, 27 & 31 (RSV)

Then God said, "Let us make man in our image, after our likeness; and let them have dominion over the fish of the sea, and over the birds of the air, and over the cattle, and over all the earth, and over every creeping thing that creeps upon the earth." [27] So God created man in his own image, in the image of God he created him; male and female he created them. . . . [31] And God saw everything that he had made, and behold, it was very good.

1. In what ways are we like God?

2. What is the significance for us in God's assessment that his creation was "very good"?

Matthew 10: 29–31 (rsv)

Are not two sparrows sold for a penny? And not one of them will fall to the ground without your Father's will. ³⁰ But even the hairs of your head are all numbered. ³¹ Fear not, therefore; you are of more value than many sparrows.

What was Jesus' purpose in comparing sparrows with human life?

Mark 8: 36 (rsv)

For what does it profit a man, to gain the whole world and forfeit his life?

The biblical teaching places more value on a single human life than secular society places on the combined wealth of all the world's oil wells.

But with this startling realization, a potential problem emerges. How can a balance be maintained between a wholesome self-concept and a genuine sense of Christian humility? (Note Rom. 12: 3.)

Mark 12: 31 (rsv)

"You shall love your neighbor as yourself."

1. What is the relationship between "self-worth" and "self-love"?

2. What is the difference between "self-love" and "selfishness"?

3. What are the subtle ways of equating sinfulness with worthlessness?

4. In our response to ourselves, what steps can we take *to understand, to accept,* and *to properly appreciate* our individual selves? How can we help each other through the same process?

5. What is the effect of healthy self-love on our ability to love the people in our lives?

6. We tend to slot people and measure their worth by their usefulness. For example, many people think a doctor is worth more than a laborer . . . a person working for a living is worth more than someone else on welfare . . . that a law-abiding citizen is worth more than a law-breaking criminal.
   What are the dangers of measuring people's worth by the cultural value of their position?

7. Complete the following statements and share your conclusions:
   What I appreciate most about being like God is . . .

If I could wave a magic wand over myself, one of the changes I would make is . . .

As I presently view myself, I would consider that one of my strengths is . . .

Our Relationship with the People in Our Lives

Luke 10: 25–37 (rsv)

And behold, a lawyer stood up to put him to the test, saying, "Teacher, what shall I do to inherit eternal life?" [26] He said to him, "What is written in the law? How do you read?" [27] And he answered, "You shall love the Lord your God with all your heart, and with all your soul, and with all your strength, and with all your mind; and your neighbor as yourself." [28] And he said to him, "You have answered right; do this, and you will live."
[29] But he, desiring to justify himself, said to Jesus, "And who is my neighbor?" [30] Jesus replied, "A man was going down from Jerusalem to Jericho, and he fell among robbers, who stripped him and beat him, and departed, leaving him half dead. [31] Now by chance a priest was going down that road; and when he saw him he passed by on the other side. [32] So likewise a Levite, when he came to the place and saw him, passed by on the other side. [33] But a Samaritan, as he journeyed, came to where he was; and when he saw him, he had compassion, [34] and went to him and bound up his wounds, pouring on oil and wine; then he set him on his own beast and brought him to an inn, and took care of him. [35] And the next day he took out two denarii and gave them to the innkeeper, saying, 'Take care of him; and whatever more you spend, I will repay you when I come back.' [36] Which of these three, do you think, proved neighbor

to the man who fell among the robbers?" [37] He said, "The one who showed mercy on him." And Jesus said to him, "Go and do likewise."

1. Within the group or in your own imagination, role play a TV interview with the man who was robbed.

Differing philosophies of life emerge from the parable. The robbers lived with the attitude that "What's yours is mine, and I'm going to take it." The priest and Levite were ruled by a selfish and a safety-first mind set. They contended that "What's mine is mine, and I'm going to keep it," while the Good Samaritan was motivated at another level. He believed that "What's mine is ours, and I'm going to share it."

2. What reasons do you think the priest and Levite would offer for refusing to help the wounded man?

3. The Samaritan faced the exact situation as those who had refused involvement. Why do you think he chose to become involved?

4. List the specific things the Samaritan did to express his love and concern toward the suffering man.

5. The lawyer was uncomfortable with Jesus' response that people are to love God, themselves and also their neighbor. Based on Jesus' response to the lawyer, who is your neighbor?

6. Thinking in a broad sense about the people who make up your life, list five individuals whom you consider to be your neighbor.

7. What *needs* do you see in the lives of these people? Be specific.

8. In what ways do we tend to rationalize our noninvolvement with the "neighbors" in our lives? Are we really different from the priest and Levite?

9. What choices do you face that will result in a developing lifestyle of involvement and love?

10. How can you specifically express your interest and love toward those five people?

Our Relationship with Our World

How big is your world? Are your borders limited to family and friends? Perhaps you reach out with your mind to include the people with whom you share your citizenship or skin color?

God's world is big. It includes all seven continents and reaches beyond the territory marked on our globes. He has no partiality to skin color. He speaks every language in his world fluently. The startling reality for those of us who are members of God's family is that we are citizens of that same world. Our world is God's world, and God's world is our world. Our world citizenship is something we should take seriously.

Our world is beautiful. Love and laughter help it dance. Humanitarian concern chases away pain. Creativity makes old ways new and fresh. Relationships remove the fear of living alone. Our world is beautiful.

But all is not beautiful in our world. Disparity and injustice rule with crushing reality. Selfishness guarantees behavior motivated by greed. Exploitation of the poor and weak often passes unchallenged. Racism quietly smokescreens dehumanization. Hunger and other forms of suffering are so rampant that indifference is generated. All is not beautiful in our world.

Jesus developed a strategy for his followers to stamp out ugliness and bring back beauty into our world. If we follow the strategy we will fulfill our world citizenship responsibilities.

Matthew 25: 31–46 (RSV)

When the Son of man comes in his glory, and all the angels with him, then he will sit on his glorious throne. [32] Before him will be gathered all the nations, and he will separate them one from another as a shepherd separates the sheep from the goats, [33] and he will place the sheep at his right hand, but the goats at the left. [34] Then the King will say to those at his right hand, "Come, O blessed of my Father, inherit the kingdom prepared for you from the foundation of the world; [35] for I was hungry and you gave me food, I was thirsty and you gave me drink, I was a stranger and you welcomed me, [36] I was naked and you clothed me, I was sick and you visited me, I was in prison and you came to me." [37] Then the righteous will answer him, "Lord, when did we see thee hungry and feed thee, or thirsty and give thee drink: [38] And when did we see thee a stranger and welcome thee, or naked and clothe thee? [39] And when did we see thee sick or in prison and visit thee?" [40] And the King will answer them, "Truly, I say to you, as you did it to one of the least of these my brethren, you did it to me." [41] Then he will say to those at his left hand, "Depart from me, you cursed, into the eternal fire prepared for the devil and his angels; [42] for I was hungry and you gave me no food, I was thirsty and you gave me no drink, [43] I was a stranger and you did not welcome me, naked and you did not clothe me, sick and in prison and you did not visit me." [44] Then they also will answer, "Lord, when did we see thee hungry or thirsty or a stranger or naked or sick or in prison, and did not minister to thee?" [45] Then he will answer them, "Truly, I say to you, as you did it not to one of the least of these, you did it not to me." [46] And they will go away into eternal punishment, but the righteous into eternal life.

1. What specific examples does Jesus give indicating how we are to respond to human need? (vv. 35–36)

2. What is the result of responding to people's needs? (vv. 37–40)

3. What is the result of refusing to respond to people's needs? (vv. 41–46)

4. The teaching of the passage is clear. " . . . As you did it to one of the least of these my brethren, you did it to me" (v. 40, RSV). In other words, when you observe needs in people's lives and respond with appropriate action to alleviate those needs, you are serving Christ.

The people needs in our world are staggering. For example, focus your mind on Bangladesh. Malnutrition and starvation are literally killing our fellow world citizens there. Contrast that situation with North America where many people are trying to cope with the crisis of losing weight in order to avoid heart attacks.

When you think about these horrendous and complex issues,

what is your response? Choose one of the following suggestions and discuss the reasons for your selection:

___I have enough trouble handling my own life.

___The problems are too big and too complex to solve.

___I'd like to help but I don't know how.

___The government should take care of the problems.

___My Christian commitment demands I do something.

Other___

5. On a television interview, Jacque Vanier astutely observed: "Perhaps the question should not be 'Why does God
permit people to starve?' but 'Why Does God permit the rich
not to share?' " What is your reaction to that statement?

6. In some measure, our ability to respond to needs in our
world is tied to the amount we spend on our self-interests. A
sociologist's survey indicated that in 1900, people in North
America lived with 18 needs and 72 desires. By 1970, the needs
had accelerated to 96, while the desires had orbited to 496.

What criteria can we develop to help us distinguish between our real needs and personal desires?

7. Having studied Jesus' statement of truth and faced the issues involved, will your life be any different? Why? Why not? How?

3. The Bible Meets You Where You Are
Sorting Out God's Teaching . . .

Love

Sin

Belief

Doubt

Love

Love may still make the "world go 'round," but for too many, love is simply the exchange of a friendly feeling or the stimulation of an erotic sensation. Followers of Jesus cannot accept such conclusions about love in their thinking or behavior.

For the Christian, love is much more than two people emotionally and physically pulled toward each other. Love is a command. Love is an attitude. Love is a choice. Love is a lifestyle. And for the Christian, Jesus is a model of what it is to love with both his words and his life.

Matthew 22: 34–40 (rsv)

> But when the Pharisees heard that he had silenced the Sadducees, they came together. [35] And one of them, a lawyer, asked him a question, to test him. [36] "Teacher, which is the great commandment in the law?" [37] And he said to him, "You shall love the Lord your God with all your heart, and with all your soul, and with all your mind. [38] This is the great and first commandment, [39] And a second is like it, You shall love your neighbor as yourself. [40] On these two commandments depend all the law and the prophets."

1. If you obey the great commandment as stated by Jesus, whom will you love?

2. God commands his people "to love." For the Christian, there is no choice . . . no substitute . . . no option . . . The Christian chooses to obey the command. The Christian does what God tells him to do whether he feels like doing it or not!

Discuss the relationship between Christian love as a command from God and the expression of that same love as an emotion or feeling.

3. The origin of love is God. The flow of Christian love is circular and continuous. God's people are only able to love because of Christ's resources in them.

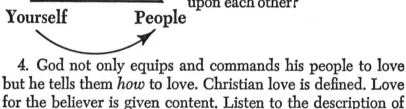

In what ways are love for God, love for yourself, and love for the people in your life dependent upon each other?

4. God not only equips and commands his people to love but he tells them *how* to love. Christian love is defined. Love for the believer is given content. Listen to the description of love from 1 Corinthians 13: 4–7 (RSV and Phillips).

> Love is patient and kind; love is not jealous or boastful; [5] it is not arrogant or rude. Love does not insist on its own way; it is not irritable or resentful; [6] it does not rejoice at wrong, but rejoices in the right. (RSV) [7] Love knows no limit to its endurance, no end to its trust, no fading of its hope; it can outlast anything. Love never fails. (Phillips)

5. What would be some of the consequences if everyone in society, everyone on the job, everyone in your church, and everyone in your family, lived the life of love as described in the above passage?

Society?

Job?

Church?

Family?

6. What would be some of the results if *you* were to express more consistently the life of love toward the people in your life? In your neighborhood?

On your job?

In your church?

In your school?

In your family?

PERSONAL LOVE TEST

Acknowledging that Christian love flows from God, is commanded, defined, and both willfully and unconditionally expressed, take a personal inventory. Rate yourself in comparison with the biblical description of love.

In response to each of the fourteen qualities of love that are listed in 1 Corinthians 13: 4–7, identify where you are in your relationship with God and your process of development by putting the appropriate letter beside each statement.

    A = Dismal Failure
    B = Sometimes But Inconsistent
    C = Still Needs Improvement
    D = Strong and Consistent

_____ 1. LOVE IS SLOW TO LOSE PATIENCE
I am content to wait without becoming angry when others fall below the expectations I have set for them.

_____ 2. LOVE IS KIND AND CONSTRUCTIVE
I am cautious in my judgments of others and honestly seek to be a healing rather than a hurting presence in my relationships.

_____ 3. LOVE IS NOT POSSESSIVE
I don't have to be in control of conversations and other situations.

_____ 4. LOVE IS NOT ANXIOUS TO IMPRESS
I can relax with who I am and don't have to be the life of the party to feel secure.

_____ 5. LOVE IS NOT ARROGANT AND EGOCENTRIC
I don't have an inflated view of my own importance and often find myself concerned about the well being of others.

_____ 6. LOVE HAS GOOD MANNERS
I respect the rights and dignity of others enough not to force my crude and thoughtless behavior on them.

_____ 7. LOVE IS NOT SELFISH
I'm not always concerned about the rights of me, myself, and I, and find pleasure in others' happiness and success.

_____ 8. LOVE IS NOT TOUCHY AND RESENTFUL
I try to understand others when they hurt me and

refuse to let hostile feelings generate toward them.

_____ 9. LOVE FINDS NO DELIGHT IN THE SIN AND SHORTCOM-
INGS OF OTHERS
I don't have to reflect on the flaws in other people
in order to rest easy with myself.

_____10. LOVE REJOICES WHEN RIGHT REIGNS AND TRUTH PRE-
VAILS
I get excited when injustices are corrected and
am angry enough to pay the price of involvement
when someone's rights are violated.

_____11. LOVE HAS STAYING POWER UNDER PRESSURE
I persevere when the easier route is to abandon
someone I was once committed to.

_____12. LOVE EXTENDS THE BENEFIT OF THE DOUBT
I discount the validity of rumors and gossip and
continue to believe the best about people until
facts prove otherwise.

_____13. LOVE SEES WITH EYES OF HOPE
I'm captivated by the potential in people and am
very much aware that what they are is not what
they can be.

_____14. LOVE REFUSES TO QUIT
When I'm tempted to throw in the towel on a person or cause, I pray for a second wind and hang
tough to the end.

Go back through the fourteen statements and substitute the
word *God* for *love*.

Go back through the fourteen statements one more time.
Substitute your own name in place of the word *love*.

PRAY like mad for Christ's resources and both a larger capacity and a stronger will *to love* God, yourself, and the people in your life.

Sin

Sin is a feeling word. Think about sin . . . talk about sin . . . and emotional reactions are guaranteed. For some, the thought of sin triggers memories of delight and the desire to do it again. Others are flooded with guilt and despair. Your reaction may be one of indifference which pushes the point of view that sin is a non-issue in our time.

The Bible's teaching about sin is both specific and comprehensive. Consider the following passages:

1 John 5: 17 (RSV)

All wrongdoing is sin . . .

The sin boundaries are wide. All behavior that is wrongdoing is sin. All unrighteousness (unrightness) is sin. Sin is knowing right and doing wrong.

1 John 3: 4 (RSV)

Everyone who commits sin is guilty of lawlessness; sin is lawlessness.

Sin is an act—an act of lawlessness. It is knowing God's law and living as a law unto oneself. Sin is doing your own thing in opposition to God's thing.

James 4: 17 (RSV)

Whoever knows what is right to do and fails to do it, for him it is sin.

Sin is refusing to act—the act of not acting. It is hearing God's instructions and knowing God's way without responding with appropriate action. Sin is knowing right and doing nothing.

Matthew 22: 37–39 (RSV)

> You shall love the Lord your God with all your heart, and with all your soul, and with all your mind. [38] This is the great and first commandment. [39] And a second is like it, You shall love your neighbor as yourself.

If God's command is "to love," and sin is "knowing what is right to do and failing to do it," then *sin is failure to love.*

Based on the biblical understanding of sin, it is no wonder the Scriptures conclude, "All have sinned and fall short of the glory of God" (Rom. 3: 23 RSV).

1. My reaction to the subject of sin is that (choose two and discuss the reasons for your selections):

_____ It belongs in a museum with other outdated relics from the past.

_____ God made us the way we are—our sin is his responsibility.

_____ Everyone has weaknesses. . . . We should simply accept each other without judging.

_____ It is the number one problem in our society—in our world.

_____ Our behavior is controlled by our past experience and present environment—so I can't be personally responsible.

_____ I believe Jesus Christ is the answer to the problem.

_____ I'm confused and not sure what I think.

2. Reflect carefully on Colossians 3: 5–15 (rsv).

Put to death therefore what is earthly in you: immorality, impurity, passion, evil desire, and covetousness, which is idolatry. [6] On account of these the wrath of God is coming. [7] In these you once walked, when you lived in them. [8] But now put them all away: anger, wrath, malice, slander, and foul talk from your mouth. [9] Do not lie to one another, seeing that you have put off the old nature with its practices [10] and have put on the new nature, which is being renewed in knowledge after the image of its creator. . . .

[12] Put on then, as God's chosen ones, holy and beloved, compassion, kindness, lowliness, meekness, and patience, [13] forbearing one another and, if one has a complaint against another, forgiving each other; as the Lord has forgiven you, so you also must forgive. [14] And above all these put on love, which binds everything together in perfect harmony. [15] And let the peace of Christ rule in your hearts, to which indeed you were called in the one body. And be thankful.

3. The passage includes a partial description of the *life of sin* and the *life of love*. List and contrast the expressions of each lifestyle.

LIFE OF SIN	LIFE OF LOVE

4. The nature and expression of sin is both internal and external. Sin manifests itself hidden inside us as well as being demonstrated outwardly. Analyze the *eleven* examples of sin listed in the passage and categorize them as follows:

INTERNAL	EXTERNAL	INTERNAL AND EXTERNAL

5. The above illustrates how sin is seen and unseen—overt and hidden. As a result, a problem can emerge. Hypocrisy can be the consequence of controlling your external behavior while hiding your real internal thoughts and feelings. How can one avoid this hypocrisy trap and live a consistent and integrated life? What should be the ideal relationship between one's internal life and external life?

6. This passage refers to our putting off the old nature and putting on the new nature so that the peace of Christ can rule in our hearts. What place does Christ's life, death, and resurrection play in our becoming *new* and being at *peace?* (Note: Luke 19: 10; Col. 3: 1–4; and Rom. 5: 1–11.)

7. What is our role in exchanging the life of sin for the life of love? (Note: 2 Cor. 7: 10; John 14: 1; 1 John 1: 9; and Phil. 4: 1.)

8. What is the condition of your present relationship with Jesus Christ?

Belief

Everyone believes something. Either by conscious choice or by unconscious default, we all live with our personal set of biases. There is no escaping a commitment to some system of thought—some ideology or philosophy of life.

What you believe will be announced by how you live. If you believe people are important you will treasure your relationships and respond to them with care and awareness. If you believe money provides the promise of the fulfilled life, you will invest your energy and creativity in accumulating as many dollars as possible. If you believe God really exists and deserves jurisdiction over your life, you will bow your will to his and let him rule.

Many voices in our society are pleading overtly and subtly: "Believe in me, and end your search for happiness! Buy me, and experience the good life! Come unto me, and find your real self—full and free!" So what else is new under the sun?

The same phenomenon was well entrenched in Paul's culture almost 2000 years ago. More details are available in Acts 17: 16–32.

Acts 17: 16–32 (rsv)

Now while Paul was waiting for them at Athens, his spirit was provoked within him as he saw that the city was full of idols. [17] So he argued in the synagogue with the Jews and the devout persons, and in the market place every day with those who chanced to be there. [18] Some also of the Epicurean and Stoic philosophers met him. And some said, "What would this babbler say?" Others said, "He seems to be a preacher of foreign divinities"—because he preached Jesus and the resurrection. [19] And they took hold of him and brought him to the Areopagus, saying, "May we know what this new teaching is which you present? [20] For you bring some strange things to our ears; we wish to know therefore what these things mean." [21] Now all the Athenians and the foreigners who lived there spent their time in nothing except telling or hearing something new.

[22] So Paul, standing in the middle of the Areopagus, said: "Men of Athens, I perceive that in every way you are very religious. [23] For as I passed along, and observed the objects of your worship, I found also an altar with this inscription, 'To an unknown god.' What therefore you worship as unknown, this I proclaim to you. [24] The God who made the world and everything in it, being Lord of heaven and earth, does not live in shrines made by man, [25] nor is he served by human hands, as though he needed anything, since he himself gives to all men life and breath and everything. [26] And he made from one every nation of men to live on all the face of the earth, having determined allotted periods and the boundaries of their habitation, [27] that they should seek God, in the hope that they might feel after him and find him. Yet he is not far from each one of us, [28] for

'In him we live and move and have our being';

as even some of your poets have said,
'For we are indeed his offspring.'

[29] Being then God's offspring, we ought not to think that the Deity is like gold, or silver, or stone, a representation by the art and imagination of man. [30] The times of ignorance God overlooked, but now he commands all men everywhere to repent, [31] because he has fixed a day on which he will judge the world in righteousness by a man whom he has appointed, and of this he has given assurance to all men by raising him from the dead."

[32] Now when they heard of the resurrection of the dead, some mocked; but others said, "We will hear you again about this."

1. Reflect on your society—your world. As you observe life around you, what idols are being worshiped in our modern world? List at least 12.

1.	7.
2.	8.
3.	9.
4.	10.
5.	11.
6.	12.

2. Paul's reaction to false god worship in the city of Athens was to become troubled, and distressed, and provoked (v. 16). Think about the modern god gallery you just listed. Think about Paul's reaction to the conditions in his culture. What is your reaction to the same scene in our time? Choose one of the following and discuss the reasons for your selection.

_____ I mind my own business and take care of my own affairs.

_____ I lack the confidence in what I believe to share it with anyone else.

_____ I don't think I have the right to challenge what other people believe.

_____ I'm with Paul. I aggressively try to gain a hearing and jump at the opportunities to represent my beliefs.

_____ Paul's style is too strong for me. I'm content to let my life speak and occasionally share what I believe with my lips.

Other ___

3. Why do you think Paul reacted the way he did?

4. As a result of Paul's distress and concern, he took action (vv. 17–21). What did he end up doing?

5. In response to the conditions in your world, what are some possible strategies for your own action?

6. Paul's condensed message to the men of Athens is really a summation of the gospel. Study verses 22–31. Isolate and list the components of Paul's message.

    1.

    2.

3.

4.

5.

6.

7.

8.

9.

10.

7. What is your personal response to the message? Are there some claims you don't understand? Are there some points that cause you to react? What makes the message unbelievable or believable to you?

8. What are the three audience responses to the claims of the message (vv. 32–34)?
   1.

   2.

   3.

9. Are the responses any different today? Why? Why not?

10. In the light of circumstances in our world and the evidence supporting the Christian message, why do you think most people continue to disbelieve rather than believe?

11. If you are a Christian—a disciple of Jesus Christ—how can you influence people to accept rather than reject God and his ways?

Doubt

Doubt doesn't have to be described for us. We know about it. We have experienced the power of doubt in us. We have tasted those haunting hunches that threaten our peace of mind. We have felt the impact of doubt deep in the pit of our stomachs when our confidence has been shattered. We have seen doubt in the arena of relationships wield its sword of destruction. We have watched doubt in a husband's faithfulness annihilate a marriage. We have seen doubt in a friend's integrity wipe out a treasured relationship. We have looked with horror as doubt has crushed what once was a dynamic faith in the person of Jesus Christ. And in our intimate moments with ourselves, we have had some questions we have been afraid to ask for fear of being attacked by that same dreaded disease.

Doubt—it stalks its victim, waiting to strike and destroy. And for many, doubt is a constant companion. It will not go away. But even in the gloom there is good news. There is honesty in God's Word. There is a doctrine of doubt.

In our discovery of the doctrine of doubt, our focus will be on a person—a notable personality in Christian history. His name is John the Baptist. For a better understanding of the significant events in his life, read the background passages in Mark 1: 1–11, John 1: 19–37, and Matthew 14: 1–12.

Two years before Jesus began his ministry, John the Baptist was out in the wilderness thundering the message of sin and repentance. Crowds came . . . many believed and repented . . . mass baptisms were the norm . . . and loyal disciples began to follow John. But since his mission was to "prepare the way of the Lord," John was ready to play second fiddle and point his disciples toward Jesus. The natural result was that John's following melted away.

During his time of center stage ministry, John had denounced the adultery that was going on in Herod's palace. His defense of truth and principle was costly. John ended up in jail. And it was down in the dungeon that John's mind played tricks on him. Satan attacked and doubt seeped into his system. John became unsure about Jesus and the whole purpose for which he had given his life.

Matthew 11: 2–11 (RSV)

Now when John heard in prison about the deeds of the Christ, he sent word by his disciplies [3] and said to him [Jesus], "Are you he who is to come, or shall we look for another?" [4] And Jesus answered them, "Go and tell John what you hear and see: [5] the blind receive their sight and the lame walk, lepers are cleansed and the deaf hear, and the dead are raised up, and the poor have good news preached to them. [6] And blessed is he who takes no offense at me."

[7] As they went away, Jesus began to speak to the crowds concerning John: "What did you go out into the wilderness to behold? A reed shaken by the wind? [8] Why then did you go out? To see a man clothed in soft raiment? Behold, those who wear soft raiment are in kings' houses. [9] Why then did you go out? To see a prophet? Yes, I tell you, and more than a prophet. [10] This is he of whom it is written,

'Behold, I send my messenger before thy face,
who shall prepare thy way before thee.'

[11] Truly, I say to you, among those born of women there has risen no one greater than John the Baptist. . . ."

1. Under the same circumstances, if I were John the Baptist in prison, I would have . . . (Select one and discuss your choice.)

_____ Kept my mouth shut and suffered in silence.

_____ Demanded a personal visit from Jesus.

_____ Done what John the Baptist did.

_____ Sent Jesus a letter complaining about my unjust treatment.

Other __

2. John lost perspective in prison—a very human thing to do. What action did John take in an attempt to cope with his doubt and concern?

3. John's action revealed his doubt and concern. What potential risks and consequences were involved in the action John took?

4. What potential risks and consequences do we run if we doubt and choose to reveal our real selves?

5. How did Jesus react to John and his request?

6. If you were Jesus in that situation, how might you have reacted?

7. Jesus responded to John with understanding and acceptance, reassurance and affirmation. Jesus' compliment to John is a treasured statement. What steps will we have to take if we choose to respond to each other in the same way?

8. Reflect on your present relationship with Jesus Christ. Estimate the level of your belief and faith in him. Indicate on the percentage line where you are *now* with an *n*, and where you would *like to be* with an *x*.

DOUBT—BELIEF

| 0% | 25% | 50% | 75% | 100% |

9. Discuss the ways we can decrease our doubt and increase our faith. What can we learn from John the Baptist in this regard? How can we respond to our doubt in a constructive manner? How can you move from where you are now to where you want to be?

4. The Bible Meets You Where You Are
Striving for the Good Life . . .

Success

Competition

Values

Security

Success

SUCCESS . . . SUCCESS . . . SUCCESS . . . like a throbbing beat that won't quit, I dream about it, I strive for it, and I am driven toward it.

Every day I live, I'm attacked by advertising agencies, peer group pressure, society's standards, my family's needs, and my self ambition to succeed!

Sometimes I get tired and want to quit but the threat of failure drives me on. I push harder, scramble to move up, and still fall short of fulfillment. Yesterday's accomplishments are never enough to satisfy today's desires.

Occasionally I slow down and stop to think. I make contact with God and he patiently helps me get my act together. We talk about success. God has his point of view and I have mine. And slowly we are becoming one.

1. From your observations, what are the criteria for success from both the secular and Christian points of view?

SECULAR WORLD CRITERIA	CHRISTIAN CRITERIA

2. Are the two views incompatible?

3. Is there anything necessarily wrong with a Christian being successful in a secular sense? Why? Why not? Under what conditions?

Joshua 1: 1–9 (rsv)

After the death of Moses the servant of the Lord, the Lord said to Joshua the son of Nun, Moses' minister, ² "Moses my servant is dead; now therefore arise, go over this Jordan, you and all this people, into the land which I am giving to them, to the people of Israel. ³ Every place that the sole of your foot will tread upon I have given to you, as I promised to Moses. ⁴ From the wilderness and this Lebanon as far as the great river, the river Euphrates, all the land of the Hittites to the Great Sea toward the going down of the sun shall be your territory. ⁵ No man shall be able to stand before you all the days of your life; as I was with Moses, so I will be with you; I will not fail you or forsake you. ⁶ Be strong and of good courage; for you shall cause this people to inherit the land which I swore to their fathers to give them. ⁷ Only be strong and very courageous, being careful to do according to all the law which Moses my servant commanded you; turn not from it to the right hand or to the left, that you may have good success wherever you go. ⁸ This book of the law shall not depart out of your mouth, but you shall meditate on it day and night, that you may be careful to do according to all that is written in it; for then you shall make your way prosperous, and then you shall have good success. ⁹ Have I not commanded you? Be strong and of good courage; be not frightened, neither be dismayed; for the Lord your God is with you wherever you go."

Moses is dead. . . . An era has passed. . . . Joshua is the new leader. . . . Uncertainty is in the atmosphere. . . .

1. How do you think Joshua viewed his new assignment? Judging from God's instructions to him, what feelings were probably churning inside him?

2. What commands did God give Joshua to obey? What promises did God offer to Joshua?

COMMANDS	PROMISES

3. According to the teaching of verses 7 and 8, how does God measure success?

What then is God's criteria for failure?

God's views on success are radical and out of step with our society. Does your personal view of success agree or disagree with God's perspective?

4. We have discovered that God equates success with knowing and obeying his instructions to us. Do you consider

God's instructions and commandments to be reasonable and justified as they apply to your life?

What factors sometimes hinder your successful response to God?

How can these hindrances be removed?

5. As you think about what is involved in being successful in the Christian sense while living in a non-Christian world, what feelings begin to churn inside you?

Competition

COMPETITION—that motivator to achieve . . . that urge to win . . . that drive to be number one . . .

Competition is one of our take-it-for-granted commodities of life. We see it, touch it, taste it, and feel it every day. But how much do we think about it in a Christian sense? Let's raise the issue and ask, is competition a vice or a virtue, a friend or an enemy?

Who would deny the value of competition? It is, after all, a trigger of initiative—a motivating force to get us moving. Competition can bring out our personal best and be a stimulator of excellence. Competition also confronts negative attitudes by fighting laziness, challenging complacency, and defeating the desire to quit.

But can we blindly applaud all that competition produces? Obviously, competition can be misused:

To stimulate hate and hamper relationships,

To instill the desire to hurt and destroy an opponent,
To stifle sensitivity about the needs of a competitor,
To justify the compromise of winning at any cost, and
To generate an inner spirit of envy when you're not
number one.

An enlightening display of group dynamics involving competition took place between Jesus, his disciples, and the mother of James and John.

Matthew 20: 17–28 (RSV)

And as Jesus was going up to Jerusalem, he took the twelve disciples aside, and on the way he said to them, [18] "Behold, we are going up to Jerusalem; and the Son of man will be delivered to the chief priests and scribes, and they will condemn him to death, [19] and deliver him to the Gentiles to be mocked and scourged and crucified, and he will be raised on the third day."

[20] Then the mother of the sons of Zebedee came up to him with her sons, and kneeling before him she asked him for something. [21] And he said to her, "What do you want?" She said to him, "Command that these two sons of mine may sit, one at your right hand and one at your left, in your kingdom." [22] But Jesus answered, "You do not know what you are asking. Are you able to drink the cup that I am to drink?" They said to him, "We are able." [23] He said to them, "You will drink my cup, but to sit at my right hand and at my left is not mine to grant, but it is for those for whom it has been prepared by my Father." [24] And when the ten heard it, they were indignant at the two brothers. [25] But Jesus called them to him and said, "You know that the rulers of the Gentiles lord it over them, and their great men exercise authority over them. [26] It shall not be so among you; but whoever would be great among you must be your servant, [27] and whoever would be first among you must be your slave; [28] even as the Son of man came not to be served but to serve, and to give his life as a ransom for many."

1. Re-create the scene. Focus on the ten disciples, the mother, Jesus and the two brothers. Gather data. Observe what you hear, see and feel about their words, attitudes and actions. Think about what motivated their actions and behavior. Attempt to measure and breathe the atmosphere that was there.

2. What human traits and drives are demonstrated in the relationships between the people involved?

3. Jesus had just talked about his death—a most serious matter! How did the disciples respond to Jesus?

4. If you had been one of the disciples there with Jesus, how would you have reacted to James and John and their mother?

5. Why do we compete?

6. In what ways do we compete?

7. In what ways do we tend to attach winning with superiority and losing with inferiority?

8. In what compartment of your life are you presently most competitive? (home, school, job, church, etc.)

Is the situation helpful or harmful to you personally? How? Why?

Is the situation helpful or harmful to the people involved in the situation with you? How? Why?

Values

I struggle converting my values from theory into practice. For example, I believe people are worth more than things, but sometimes things push people aside and come out on top. Sometimes I find myself thinking and saying one thing and doing something that is really contradictory such as loudly singing, "I'd rather have Jesus than silver and gold . . ." and then spending the energy of my life piling up the perishable. That gap between my lips and my life troubles me. Could it be that we sometimes have two sets of values? Values we talk about and others we live by? Our theoretical values and our real-life values? I'm not sure, but I do know that I don't like me very much when inconsistency rules.

Valuing Your Values: A very private encounter with the real you.
    What is important to you?

What priorities direct your life?

How do you measure your treasures?

If you were able to wave a magic wand and order the details of your life, what would you create?

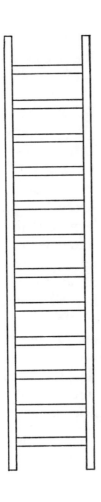

Study the list below by yourself. Place the number of your most treasured value on the top rung of the ladder. Place the number of the least appealing value on the bottom rung. Arrange the other values on the rungs in between the highest and lowest in the order in which you would rate them. And—BE HONEST!

1. A clear mortgage on your dream home
2. Social status and prestigious friends
3. Leisure time and freedom to use it as you choose
4. A healthy marriage and a stable home
5. Physical beauty and sex appeal
6. Ph.D. degree from a notable university
7. Christ's love and God's acceptance
8. Physical and emotional health
9. Executive chair in your own prosperous business
10. Resources to contribute to others' needs
11. Guarantee of faithful friends
12. An inner self at rest and peace

Philippians 4: 8–9 (RSV)

Finally, brethren, whatever is true, whatever is honorable, whatever is just, whatever is pure, whatever is lovely, what-

ever is gracious, if there is any excellence, if there is anything worthy of praise, think about these things. ⁹ What you
have learned and received and heard and seen in me, do;
and the God of peace will be with you.

2 Peter 1: 3–11 (RSV)

His divine power has granted to us all things that pertain
to life and godliness, through the knowledge of him who
called us to his own glory and excellence, ⁴ by which he has
granted to us his precious and very great promises, that
through these you may escape from the corruption that is in
the world because of passion, and become partakers of the
divine nature. ⁵ For this very reason make every effort to
supplement your faith with virtue, and virtue with knowledge, ⁶ and knowledge with self-control, and self-control with
steadfastness, and steadfastness with godliness, ⁷ and godliness with brotherly affection, and brotherly affection with
love. ⁸ For if these things are yours and abound, they keep
you from being ineffective or unfruitful in the knowledge
of our Lord Jesus Christ. ⁹ For whoever lacks these things
is blind and shortsighted and has forgotten that he was
cleansed from his old sins. ¹⁰ Therefore, brethren, be the
more zealous to confirm your call and election, for if you
do this you will never fall; ¹¹ so there will be richly provided
for you an entrance into the eternal kingdom of our Lord
and Savior Jesus Christ.

1. List the fourteen values and virtues established by God
in these passages.

2. Go back through the list and identify a form of behavior

that would be a practical expression of each value. For example:

> TRUTH: Publicly defending the principle that "a man's life does not consist in the abundance of possessions" (Luke 12: 15, RSV) by refusing to let the gaining of money rule your decision-making.

3. Review the list of values again. Identify two areas where you feel you are personally excelling. Identify two other areas where you feel you need to improve.

4. What is your reaction to Paul's statement: "What you have . . . seen in me, do"?

5. What do the Scriptures indicate will be the *results* of developing and practicing the values listed in the two passages?

6. Go back to your ladder of values. After gaining a biblical perspective on what is important, are there some adjustments you need to make in your thinking and doing? How will you make those changes?

Security

The seams of our social system are unraveling. Governments have broken trust and are scrambling to establish credibility. Inflation is threatening our standard of living. The energy crisis is crimping our lifestyles. Marriage is only an ugly memory for too many. Disregard for authority justifies new forms of anarchy. Unemployment is hanging over many like a guillotine ready to fall. Rapid and radical change is forcing us to question whether anything is permanent anymore. The influence of the church on society is not getting stronger.

The future is cluttered with question marks. We face issues. Big issues. Concerns that matter. Whom do we trust? What can we believe in that will last? On what do we stake our lives? Where do we go to find security?

1. Project yourself into the following situations. Complete the statement, "I feel most secure . . ." (Choose two.)

____ When I am at home alone in the bathtub

____ When all my bills are paid

____ When I'm with friends who care about me

____ When I'm at church worshiping God

____ When I am busy working and achieving

____ When I'm at a stoplight in my new Oldsmobile sitting next to a 1963 Pontiac

Think about yourself and your situation indicating when you feel most insecure. Why does insecurity move in on you?

Romans 8: 31–39 (rsv)

What then shall we say to this? If God is for us, who is against us? [32] He who did not spare his own Son but gave him up for us all, will he not also give us all things with him? ³³ Who shall bring any charge against God's elect? It is God who justifies; ³⁴ who is to condemn? Is it Christ Jesus, who died, yes, who was raised from the dead, who is at the right hand of God, who indeed intercedes for us? ³⁵ Who shall separate us from the love of Christ? Shall tribulation, or distress, or persecution, or famine, or nakedness, or peril, or sword? ³⁶ As it is written,

> "For thy sake we are being killed all the day long;
> we are regarded as sheep to be slaughtered."

³⁷ No, in all these things we are more than conquerors through him who loved us. ³⁸ For I am sure that neither death, nor life, nor angels, nor principalities, nor things present, nor things to come, nor powers, ³⁹ nor height, nor depth, nor anything else in all creation, will be able to separate us from the love of God in Christ Jesus our Lord.

2. What a dramatic declaration! Paul is voicing incredible confidence. List the seventeen threats to our security that Paul contends can be overcome with a strong faith in Jesus Christ.

3. Give concrete examples for at least ten of those phenomena that are being experienced in people's lives in our time. For example, *sword*—war in the Middle East.

4. Reflecting on that list and examples, do you think Paul
____ Belongs in a mental asylum.
____ Has sold out his mind to his emotions.

_____ Is something like Jesus, too strong to be real.
_____ Really has life put together.
_____ Is totally out of contact with reality.

5. From the passage and your understanding of Paul's life and experience, what is the basis of his faith and confidence? What are the reasons he is so unthreatened and secure?

6. Does Jesus deserve as much trust as Paul gives him? Why? Why not?

7. Is Paul any different from you and me? Is he in a special category of humanity? Is his confidence and security within our reach today? Discuss your responses.

8. Secular society leans on money, status, family, friends, material possessions, government controls, job skills, retirement programs, insurance policies, and other temporal goodies for its sense of security.

The Christian is supposed to be living in that setting being a threat instead of being threatened. The believer is to refuse to let the world around him squeeze him into its own mold. That is a tough assignment.

What pressures does society exert on the Christian that tend to threaten his confidence and rob him of his security in Christ?

9. What strategy can the Christian deploy so he can acquire confidence in Christ and enjoy a strong sense of security?

5. The Bible Meets You Where You Are

Coping with Personal Despair . . .

> *Guilt*
>
> *Depression*
>
> *Loneliness*
>
> *Failure*

Guilt

Guilt is moral pain. Every person has the capacity to harbor and experience guilt.

This ability to feel convicted for wrong doing or the lack of right doing, is crucial for our survival. Guilt is like a safety valve. It protects us from moral deterioration and ethical destruction. Like sensing physical pain from a hot stove protects us from more severe injury, moral pain triggered by God and our behavior can confront and correct our unacceptable ways of living.

However, not all forms of guilt are wholesome or desirable. Guilt can torture and paralyze. Guilt can stifle and produce needless inner conflict. Be alert for false guilt—a guilt that is imposed without a valid reason. False guilt can be sheltered in truth that is distorted. It can be delivered in either a subtle or overt package through peer group pressures to conform. The destructive and damaging results of false guilt can even be transmitted by well-meaning but confused saints! Who would argue that employers and workers, parents and children, friends and acquaintances, boyfriends and girlfriends are all capable of using guilt as a tool to manipulate the people in their lives for their own selfish ends?

In the areas of ethics and morality, our society has posted detour signs around guilt trips. Permissiveness in our thinking and lifestyles has dulled our consciences to any sense of moral oughtness. We must be on guard because a guiltless society is a dangerous society.

So let's open ourselves to clear thinking and commit ourselves to honest action regarding the subject and reality of guilt.

1. Think about your life, your background, your society. What forces and influences stimulate and create guilt?

2. Distinguish between real guilt and false guilt. List examples.

2 Samuel 11 (RSV)

In the spring of the year, the time when kings go forth to battle, David sent Joab, and his servants with him, and all Israel; and they ravaged the Ammonites, and besieged Rabbah. But David remained at Jerusalem.

[2] It happened, late one afternoon, when David arose from his couch and was walking upon the roof of the king's house, that he saw from the roof a woman bathing; and the woman was very beautiful. [3] And David sent and inquired about the woman. And one said, "Is not this Bathsheba, the daughter of Eliam, the wife of Uriah the Hittite?" [4] So David sent messengers, and took her; and she came to him, and he lay with her. (Now she was purifying herself from her uncleanness.) Then she returned to her house. [5] And the woman conceived; and she sent and told David, "I am with child."

[6] So David sent word to Joab, "Send me Uriah the Hittite." And Joab sent Uriah to David. [7] When Uriah came to him, David asked how Joab was doing, and how the people fared, and how the war prospered. [8] Then David said to Uriah, "Go down to your house, and wash your feet." And Uriah went out of the king's house and there followed him a present from the king. [9] But Uriah slept at the door of the king's house with all the servants of his lord, and did not go down to his house. [10] When they told David, "Uriah did not go down to his house," David said to Uriah, "Have you not come

from a journey? Why did you not go down to your house?"
[11] Uriah said to David, "The ark and Israel and Judah dwell
in booths; and my lord Joab and the servants of my lord are
camping in the open field; shall I then go to my house, to eat
and to drink, and to lie with my wife? As you live, and as
your soul lives, I will not do this thing." [12] Then David said
to Uriah, "Remain here today also, and tomorrow I will let
you depart." So Uriah remained in Jerusalem that day, and
the next. [13] And David invited him, and he ate in his presence
and drank, so that he made him drunk; and in the evening
he went out to lie on his couch with the servants of his lord,
but he did not go down to his house.

[14] In the morning David wrote a letter to Joab, and sent
it by the hand of Uriah. [15] In the letter he wrote, "Set Uriah
in the forefront of the hardest fighting, and then draw back
from him, that he may be struck down, and die." [16] And as
Joab was besieging the city, he assigned Uriah to the place
where he knew there were valiant men. [17] And the men of
the city came out and fought with Joab; and some of the
servants of David among the people fell. Uriah the Hittite was
slain also. [18] Then Joab sent and told David all the news about
the fighting; [19] and he instructed the messenger, "When you
have finished telling all the news about the fighting to the
king, [20] then, if the king's anger rises, and if he says to you,
'Why did you go so near the city to fight? Did you not know
that they would shoot from the wall? [21] Who killed Abimelech
the son of Jerubbesheth? Did not a woman cast an upper
millstone upon him from the wall, so that he died at Thebez?
Why did you go so near the wall?' then you shall say, 'Your
servant Uriah the Hittite is dead also.'"

[22] So the messenger went, and came and told David all
that Joab had sent him to tell. [23] The messenger said to David,
"The men gained an advantage over us, and came out against
us in the field; but we drove them back to the entrance of
the gate. [24] Then the archers shot at your servants from the
wall; some of the king's servants are dead; and your servant
Uriah the Hittite is dead also." [25] David said to the messenger,
"Thus shall you say to Joab, 'Do not let this matter trouble

you, for the sword devours now one and now another;
strengthen your attack upon the city, and overthrow it.' And
encourage him."

[26] When the wife of Uriah heard that Uriah her husband
was dead, she made lamentation for her husband. [27] And when
the mourning was over, David sent and brought her to his
house, and she became his wife, and bore him a son. But
the thing that David had done displeased the Lord.

1. What behavior generated David's guilt? Was his guilt
real or false? Why?

2. Choose one of the following and share the reasons for
your choice. I think David bowed to temptation and behaved
as he did with Bathsheba because:

_____ He was the king and thought he was an exception to
God's laws.

_____ His behavior was already determined by his trau-
matic childhood experiences.

_____ He was weak, human and unloving toward the people in his life.

_____ He had a hard day, and anyway, sometimes God's
standards are too high.

_____ He was selfish and sinful and thoughtless about the
lives he wrecked.

Other _____

3. What were David's three strategies for handling Uriah and covering up his wrongdoing?

4. What were the reasons Uriah did not cooperate with David's first two plots? As a result of Uriah's behavior, what can we conclude about his character?

5. David's guilt and action implicated others. General Joab became a pawn in David's hands. What can we conclude about Joab's character? In what other ways could Joab have responded to David's requests?

6. In David's conversation with the messenger, how did he attempt to justify his action and reassure Joab?

7. How should we handle our own guilt? (Discuss the reasons for your selections.)

_____ Lower our standards to the level of our behavior.

_____ Develop calloused and insensitive consciences.

_____ Vow not to repeat the wrong act a second time.

_____ Confess our wrongdoing to God and receive his forgiveness.

___ Make compensation to the persons wronged through restitution.

___ Feel sorry about our misdeeds and cover our tracks so we don't get caught.

Other ___

8. The last note in the chapter is a sad one. The Scriptures pinpoint God's reaction to the whole affair by directly stating, "The thing that David had done displeased the Lord." Substitute your own name for David's. If the Lord should be displeased with you, how serious a concern would that be to you? Why? Why not?

9. The record shows that David's attitude shifted and changed. Psalm 51 flowed from both David's pen and his life. Read the Psalm in unison. In silence, reflect on the passage's meaning and consequences. Then pray together for each other.

Depression

A few months ago, I went on a retreat—an inward retreat to despair and depression. I'm normal—even the psychiatrists would agree with that self-diagnosis!

Normal or not, the emotional crash was real. I was bound by blackness. Internal turmoil sapped my motivation and drive. My self-pity drove me to selfishness. I didn't like me very much.

There I was, living with the absence of hope, and bowing to the stifling control of inner darkness even though the summer sun was shining. Death wasn't attractive yet, but life had to have a better alternative.

You know the feeling—you've been there, too. We all have our emotional ups and downs. Our feelings are on the move. Deny the normalcy of emotional movement and depression and you are either severely sick or guilty of emotional dishonesty.

Somewhere on my retreat, I had a thought. It was profound at the time. Depression put on a new face. My insight came out this way: The emotional trip down could be healthy if the pattern of depression was within limits and was a way of coping with natural disappointment and distressing circumstances.

Something else happened. . . . God broke into the darkness. He reassured me by simply communicating, "I understand. . . . Relax. . . . Rest. . . . You are going to be all right. You are not the first of my people to suffer from depression. If you don't believe me, take a look at Elijah or Jonah, or John the Baptist.

So let's take a look at Elijah and learn from his experience. The details are found in the book of 1 Kings, chapter 19. Important background reading is in chapters 17 and 18.

1 Kings 19 (RSV)

Ahab told Jezebel all that Elijah had done, and how he had slain all the prophets with the sword. ² Then Jezebel sent a messenger to Elijah, saying, "So, may the gods do to me, and more also, if I do not make your life as the life of one of them by this time tomorrow." ³ Then he was afraid, and he arose and went for his life, and came to Beersheba, which belongs to Judah, and left his servant there.

⁴ But he himself went a day's journey into the wilderness,

and came and sat down under a broom tree; and he asked that he might die, saying, "It is enough; now, O Lord, take away my life; for I am no better than my fathers." ⁵ And he lay down and slept under a broom tree; and behold, an angel touched him, and said to him, "Arise and eat." ⁶ And he looked, and behold, there was at his head a cake baked on hot stones and a jar of water. And he ate and drank, and lay down again. ⁷ And the angel of the Lord came again a second time, and touched him, and said, "Arise and eat, else the journey will be too great for you." ⁸ And he arose, and ate and drank, and went in the strength of that food forty days and forty nights to Horeb the mount of God.

⁹ And there he came to a cave, and lodged there; and behold, the word of the Lord came to him, and he said to him, "What are you doing here, Elijah?" ¹⁰ He said, "I have been very jealous for the Lord, the God of hosts; for the people of Israel have forsaken thy covenant, thrown down thy altars, and slain thy prophets with the sword; and I, even I only, am left; and they seek my life, to take it away." ¹¹ And he said, "Go forth, and stand upon the mount before the Lord." And behold, the Lord passed by, and a great and strong wind rent the mountains, and broke in pieces the rocks before the Lord, but the Lord was not in the wind; and after the wind an earthquake, but the Lord was not in the earthquake; ¹² and after the earthquake a fire, but the Lord was not in the fire; and after the fire a still small voice. ¹³ And when Elijah heard it, he wrapped his face in his mantle and went out and stood at the entrance of the cave. And behold, there came a voice to him, and said, "What are you doing here, Elijah?" ¹⁴ He said, "I have been very jealous for the Lord, the God of hosts; for the people of Israel have forsaken thy covenant, thrown down thy altars, and slain thy prophets with the sword; and I, even I only, am left; and they seek my life, to take it away." ¹⁵ And the Lord said to him, "Go, return on your way to the wilderness of Damascus; and when you arrive, you shall anoint Hazael to be king over Syria; ¹⁶ and Jehu the son of Nimshi you shall anoint to be king over Israel; and Elisha the son of Shaphat of Abelmeholah you shall anoint

to be prophet in your place. [17] And him who escapes from the sword of Hazael shall Jehu slay; and him who escapes from the sword of Jehu shall Elisha slay. [18] Yet I will leave seven thousand in Israel, all the knees that have not bowed to Baal, and every mouth that has not kissed him."

[19] So he departed from there, and found Elisha the son of Shaphat, who was plowing, with twelve yoke of oxen before him, and he was with the twelfth. Elijah passed by him and cast his mantle upon him. [20] And he left the oxen, and ran after Elijah, and said, "Let me kiss my father and my mother, and then I will follow you." And he said to him, "Go back again; for what have I done to you?" [21] And he returned from following him, and took the yoke of oxen, and slew them, and boiled their flesh with the yokes of the oxen, and gave it to the people, and they ate. Then he arose and went after Elijah, and ministered to him.

Elijah had been enjoying the most remarkable days of his life and ministry. God was using him in humble and impressive ways. His prophetic role ranged from being a weather forecaster to giving life to a little boy who had died. Elijah's towering triumph, however, was the drama on Mount Carmel. He confidently annihilated all the prophets of Baal and clearly established that his God was in control. Elijah had been on an emotional high. He was about to crash to a record low.

1. From the passage what was the source and nature of the threat that robbed Elijah of his confidence and overwhelmed him?

2. Elijah decided to run—120 miles to Beersheba, plus another 200 miles to Mount Horeb. The threat of death was too much for him to handle. Based on the circumstances of the moment, do you think Elijah's action was reasonable and rational? Why? Why not?

3. Examine the passage again. What did Elijah conclude about himself and his circumstances? Were his conclusions correct?

4. In response to Elijah's plight, how did God respond to Elijah? What specific things did God do?

5. What value for Elijah was there in God's nonthreatening question, "What are you doing here?"

6. God understands our humanness. When Elijah was tired and hungry, God gave him rest and a hot meal. . . . When Elijah needed to vent his inner despair, God asked him an open-ended question. . . . When Elijah lost perspective and contemplated suicide, God sent him back into the battle with life. . . .

Think about the events of your life and your own behavior during the last three months. Chart your emotional movement during that period of time with a line drawing.

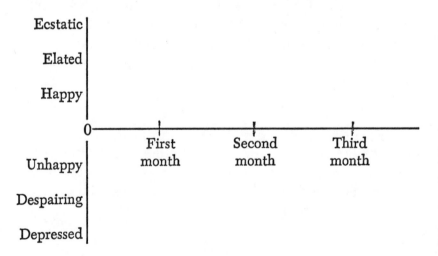

7. What can we learn from Elijah's life and experience that will be of value in understanding ourselves as we relate to others?

8. What can we conclude about God's dealing with our depression syndromes?

Loneliness

The incident you are about to read really happened. The event is historical. With one exception, the people in the drama are like you . . . ordinary . . . normal . . . at least on most days!

Jesus has the leading role. Twelve others share the stage with him. Three of the twelve give their performances under the glare of the spotlight.

In the original setting, the group had just left another heavy session. They had been together in an upstairs room—eating and drinking and talking. Dramatic and baffling announcements had been made there. Charges of impending betrayal had shocked the group. Declarations of loyalty had been proclaimed. Competition and jealousy had threatened their peace and unity. None of the group felt very secure. A fog of confusion clouded the future. But they were still together in another setting—a garden called Gethsemane.

Matthew 26: 36–46 (rsv)

> Then Jesus went with them to a place called Gethsemane, and he said to his disciples, "Sit here, while I go yonder and pray." [37] And taking with him Peter and the two sons of

Zebedee, he began to be sorrowful and troubled. [38] Then he said to them, "My soul is very sorrowful, even to death; remain here, and watch with me." [39] And going a little farther he fell on his face and prayed, "My Father, if it be possible, let this cup pass from me; nevertheless, not as I will, but as thou wilt," [40] And he came to the disciples and found them sleeping; and he said to Peter, "So, could you not watch with me one hour? [41] Watch and pray that you may not enter into temptation; the spirit indeed is willing, but the flesh is weak." [42] Again, for the second time, he went away and prayed, "My Father, if this cannot pass unless I drink it, thy will be done." [43] And again he came and found them sleeping, for their eyes were heavy. [44] So, leaving them again, he went away and prayed for the third time, saying the same words. [45] Then he came to the disciples and said to them, "Are you still sleeping and taking your rest? Behold, the hour is at hand, and the Son of man is betrayed into the hands of sinners. [46] Rise, let us be going; see, my betrayer is at hand."

1. Jesus was with his disciples, but in reality he was both alone and lonely. Distinguish between "being alone" and "being lonely."

2. Jesus was open about his internal stress—his loneliness and despair. He confesses, "My soul is very sorrowful" or "My heart is nearly breaking." What keeps us from revealing our real selves to each other?

3. In the midst of his personal struggle, Jesus invited Peter, James and John to share his crisis. When do we feel safe enough to invite others into our lives?

4. Jesus did not invite Peter, James and John into the trauma and intimacy of his life so they could go to sleep! His

three friends really deserted him. Why do we sometimes desert each other?

5. How did Jesus respond to his friends' lack of sensitivity to his crisis and need? When people fail to reach the expectations we have set for them, what options of response are available to us?

6. In dealing with his crisis, Jesus was honest with himself, shared his real self with others, and faced his Father with the facts. Reflect on the ways Jesus implemented this pattern of response.

7. Turn on the memory system in your personal computer and recall one of the loneliest experiences of your life. How did you handle the crisis? Did you follow Jesus' pattern? After observing Jesus' example, given the opportunity for a rerun, would you handle your situation differently? In what ways?

Failure

The apostle Peter, a follower of this fellow Jesus, is a model of our humanity.

He wanted to be strong but was weak.

He wanted to be faithful but was unpredictable.

He wanted to be effective but was inconsistent.

He wanted to be successful but he failed.

Peter was like you and me:

We have honorable intentions that never get expressed.

We have noble aspirations that stay beyond our reach.

We set goals that elude our capture.

We make commitments and end up breaking them.

Like Peter, we know about failure. We have tasted it. . . . We have felt the force of its power to destroy. . . . We have experienced the inner throbbing pain that failure brings to its victim.

Focus your attention on an event in Peter's life—an experience Peter would like to relive and handle differently.

Luke 22: 54–62 (RSV)

Then they seized him and led him away, bringing him into the high priest's house. Peter followed at a distance; [55] and when they had kindled a fire in the middle of the courtyard and sat down together, Peter sat among them. [56] Then a maid, seeing him as he sat in the light and gazing at him, said, "This man also was with him." [57] But he denied it, saying, "Woman, I do not know him." [58] And a little later someone else saw him and said, "You also are one of them." But Peter said, "Man, I am not." [59] And after an interval of about an hour still another insisted, saying, "Certainly this man also was with him; for he is a Galilean." [60] But Peter said, "Man, I do not know what you are saying." And immediately, while he was still speaking, the cock crowed. [61] And the Lord turned and looked at Peter. And Peter remembered the word of the Lord, how he had said to him, "Before the cock crows today; you will deny me three times." [62] And he went out and wept bitterly.

1. If you were Peter in that situation, would you have . . . (Choose one response and share the reasons for your choice.)

_____Preached a sermon

_____Failed just like Peter did

＿＿Said nothing and left quickly

＿＿Never followed Jesus in the first place

＿＿Used the opportunity for a tactful witness

Other＿

2. What were the forces and pressures in the situation that threatened Peter?

3. Just hours before his denial, Peter had shared the sacrament of the Lord's supper with Jesus, he had publically declared his allegience to faithfully follow his Lord, and he had been close to Jesus in the intimacy of the Garden of Gethsemene. But now, Peter was denying any association with this same Jesus. How do you account for the change in Peter's behavior?

4. What was Peter's reaction to himself when the event had passed?

5. What does Peter's conduct teach us about our own potential behavior?

Let's move to a later event. In the time sequence, Jesus' trial is past. His death and resurrection are history. Jesus appears on the sandy shore of the sea building a fire in preparation to cook breakfast. Peter is back on his old job with his boat and fishing nets. The morning air is chilly and the relationships are a little strained. But after a tasty breakfast and when hungry stomachs are full, Jesus and Peter talk.

John 21: 15–19 (rsv)

When they had finished breakfast, Jesus said to Simon Peter, "Simon, son of John, do you love me more than these?" He said to him, "Yes, Lord; you know that I love you." He said to him, "Feed my lambs." 16 A second time he said to him, "Simon, son of John, do you love me?" He said to him, "Yes, Lord; you know that I love you." He said to him, "Tend my sheep." 17 He said to him a third time, "Simon, son of John, do you love me?" Peter was grieved because he said to him the third time, "Do you love me?" And he said to him, "Lord, you know everything; you know that I love you." Jesus said to him, "Feed my sheep. 18 Truly, truly, I say to you, when you were young, you girded yourself and walked where you would; but when you are old, you will stretch out your hands, and another will gird you and carry you where you do not wish to go." 19 (This he said to show by what death he was to glorify God.) And after this he said to him, "Follow me."

Jesus is fully aware of Peter's past performance. But yet, there is no reminder or no "I told you so" attitude about the horror in the courtyard. Neither is there a lecture or reprimand from Jesus to Peter about being faithful and dependable.

6. What was Jesus' response to Peter? What opportunities did the open-ended question offer to Peter?

7. What does Jesus' response to Peter and his failure communicate to us about Jesus' response to our own failures?

8. Jesus was aware of the difference between "failing" and "being a failure." Distinguish between the two.

9. What is commendable about Peter's response to Jesus' questions? What might Peter have said?

10. Jesus offered the right to fail and the freedom to begin again. His last words to Peter were "Follow Me." Thinking about some of your own past failures and hearing Jesus say to you personally, "Follow Me," what failure is Jesus wanting to lead you out of? Think about yourself—your home, your job, your school, your secret, inner life. To what new venture are you being called? What is your response to the invitation?

6. The Bible Meets You Where You Are

Sharing Christ's Mission . . .

   To Contact God

   To Communicate Good News

   To Discover Freedom

   To Demonstrate the Truth

Sharing Christ's Mission

There are a few things I wish Jesus had not said. Instructions like "love your enemies . . . deny yourself . . . expect to be persecuted . . . and the rich will find it tough to get into the kingdom of God" are not exactly reasons to organize a celebration. Another surprise package Jesus left with us soon after his death and resurrection was, "As the Father has sent me, even so I send you" (John 20: 21, RSV).

How to even consider that package is to take on a heavy duty issue. Unless we can relegate this directive from Jesus as the exclusive responsibility of missionaries bound for Bangladesh, we are in deep trouble. Our trouble directly confronted is that Jesus is calling his followers to be like him. Even the thought of impersonating Jesus is intimidating to us. Deep down where our integrity resides, we know we are not like Jesus. We live with the hunch that there has only been one Jesus and that he will never be reproduced. Our inner conviction asserts that Jesus is somehow different . . . constructed out of better stuff . . . qualitatively superior . . . radically distinctive . . . new and improved and unconditionally guaranteed.

But still, we cannot get away from Jesus' mandate. The directive does rest on the shoulders of all those who choose to respond to him. To disregard the command to be like Jesus is to move away from God and that is not a Christian option. And so we move toward God, accepting the Christian mission to go into the world—thinking like Jesus, behaving like Jesus and, above all, leaving the same atmosphere of love that Jesus left when he related to a group of people or talked to an individual.

Our difficulty develops when we seriously attempt to impersonate this fellow Jesus. We discover that the phrase "be like Jesus" is not enough on which to base a lifestyle. We need more specifics . . . an elaboration . . . a clarification. In our imagination we dream about a personal update in a face to face, person to person encounter with Jesus. A weekend fishing trip would be ideal. A luncheon date to discuss the issues would be a partial solution. A telephone conversation would sort out some of the problems. Even a prime time television feature with Jesus as the special guest would help.

Back in reality, we continue to question. "How can a follower of Jesus be like his leader in our twentieth century society?" With increasing certainty, we can anticipate Jesus' response as we watch him reach for the Scriptures and listen to him redeliver his original inaugural address. From his memory, Jesus would quietly but forcefully recite the words of Isaiah 61: 1 and Luke 4: 18—

"The Spirit of the Lord is upon me, because he has anointed me to preach good news to the poor. He has sent me to proclaim release to the captives, and recovering of sight to the blind, to set at liberty those who are oppressed, to proclaim the acceptable day of the Lord."

Jesus would then open his eyes and with a faint smile on his lips and tenderness in his voice, he would say, "Here is the statement of my mission—the creed of my life. If you want to be like me in your world, you must share my mission there."

The following studies are designed to clarify and amplify the teaching and application of Jesus' mission as stated in Luke 4: 18.

To Contact God

Jesus had launched his public ministry. Rumors about this carpenter from Nazareth in Galilee were spreading. His reputation was developing. Now Jesus was heading back to Nazareth—no big homecoming, just back home—for a small family reunion and a guest appearance at the local synagogue.

Hidden between the lines of the scriptural account are intriguing snapshots of the humanity of Jesus and his normalness as a real person. As you read and discuss the event, ask yourself:

> Where do you think Jesus slept?
>
> What do you think was on the menu for supper?
>
> What topics were a part of the supper-table conversation?
>
> When the Sabbath arrived, and Jesus walked his normal route to the synagogue, whom do you think he met on the way? What did they talk about?

Luke 4: 14–18 (RSV)

> And Jesus returned in the power of the Spirit into Galilee, and a report concerning him went out through all the surrounding country. [15] And he taught in their synagogues, being glorified by all.
>
> [16] And he came to Nazareth, where he had been brought up; and he went to the synagogue, as his custom was, on the sabbath day. And he stood up to read; [17] and there was given to him the book of the prophet Isaiah. He opened the book and found the place where it was written, [18] "the Spirit of the Lord is upon me. . . . "

That Sabbath morning, Jesus' growing reputation had earned him an invitation to be the guest speaker at the syna-

gogue. Following the regular custom for worship, Jesus took
the scroll and began to read from the prophet Isaiah (chapter
61). When he had finished, he sat down and began to explain
the meaning of the passage as it applied to himself and his mission. If only a cassette tape recorder could have been switched
on.

1. When Jesus had cleared his throat and read, "The Spirit
of the Lord is upon me," what personal experience must have
rushed into his mind? (Note: Matt. 3: 13–17.) What do you
think the memory of that experience generated inside Jesus?

Our personal and desperate need rests here. We too must be
touched by God, if we are to share in Jesus' mission. Like Jesus,
our experience needs to be logged as a historical event. There
is no substitute for our making personal contact with God. A
crash course on God is not sufficient. Correct theological information is not the solution. Our need is to be touched. Our
human spirits must make contact with God's Spirit. There
must be that encounter between the Creator and the created—
that moving toward God with the response of Divine penetra-
tion . . . that coming together . . . that linking up between God
and the individual. Biblical descriptions of the miracle of spiritual birth are numerous. Consider the communication from
God in the following passage.

2 Corinthians 5: 17–21 (RSV)

Therefore, if any one is in Christ, he is a new creation; the
old has passed away, behold, the new has come. [18] All this is
from God, who through Christ reconciled us to himself and
gave us the ministry of reconciliation; [19] that is, God was in
Christ reconciling the world to himself, not counting their
trespasses against them, and entrusting to us the message of
reconciliation. [20] So we are ambassadors for Christ, God mak-

ing his appeal through us. We beseech you on behalf of Christ, be reconciled to God. [21] For our sake he made him to be sin who knew no sin, so that in him we might become the righteousness of God.

2. *On what basis* is it possible for us to make contact with God?

3. To what ministry have the "new creations in Christ" been called? What is involved in the ministry of reconciliation?

4. Think about the role of international statesmen and ambassadors from your country to other countries. What are the marks of a quality ambassador?

5. What then are the marks of a quality ambassador for God?

6. From your view of yourself, where are you today?
_____Have you been touched by God?
_____Do you have any desire or motivation to connect with God?
_____Are you active in your ministry of reconciliation?
_____How do you rate the quality of your ambassadorship?
Does the thought of sharing Jesus' mission:
_____attract you?
_____intimidate you?
_____scare you?
_____leave you cold?

To Communicate Good News

My teenage memories about the gospel and churchianity are not exactly inspiring to recall. The Bible was a rule book. God was an austere judge enforcing the rules. The church was like a courthouse handing down the judge's verdicts. My rebellious nature meant I spent a lot of time grounded and unable to follow my selfish pursuits. Frankly, God and his gospel were *bad news*—narrow, negative and restrictive!

Fortunately, I began to grow up a little and my perceptions did change. The Bible became a trustworthy document accurately stating God's truth. God emerged as a friend instead of a foe. I remember the shock when I suddenly saw that God was concerned about my best interests. As far as getting the church scene together, well, I'm still trying to work that one out. My nature is still a bit rebellious but I'm aware of how damaging and destructive following my selfish pursuits can be for me and the people who share my life. Thankfully, today, God and his gospel are *good news*—liberating, freeing, and enabling!

I was a little surprised to look around at North American society and discover, that for most people, God and his gospel were neither good news nor bad news, but rather *no news* at all! One can't help but be distressed by the realization that the majority of people have concluded that if God exists, he doesn't matter . . . that the Christian Church is a non-issue . . . that the Bible can be disregarded . . . and that the gospel is a nothing—a big zero!

1. Think about the issues involved. What ingredients make the difference?

Why is the gospel "good news"?

When does the gospel become "bad news"?

What factors have contributed to make the gospel "no news"?

Remember that we are seeking a better understanding of Jesus' mission so that we can more effectively pursue the Christian's mission in society. So in our identification with Jesus, we too must conclude: "The Spirit of the Lord is upon me, *because he has anointed me to preach good news to the poor . . ."* (Luke 4: 18, rsv).

2. Preaching is a mode of communication. What are the various ways we communicate information and give impressions to other people about God and his gospel?

3. Jesus' life was a demonstration of the words he spoke. His behavior was the bridge between his theory and practice. What obstacles stand in the way of our living with that same consistency between what we say and what we do?

4. Jesus' method of communicating the good news was to take his clues from the individual and the specific situation at hand. In practice, Jesus' response to Zacchaeus (Luke 19: 1–10) was radically different from his response to Nicodemus (John 3: 1–15), the rich young ruler (Mark 10: 17–22), the woman at the well (John 4: 1–30), and the 5,000 who were hungry (John 6: 1–14).

Is Jesus' methodology in sharing the gospel one we should attempt to duplicate? Why? Why not?

What personal steps will we have to move through before we are in a position to follow the pattern demonstrated by Jesus?

5. When you think about personally communicating the gospel, what response generates inside you? (Choose one of the following.)

_____I develop a failure complex

_____I stay relaxed and do what comes naturally

_____I get defensive and insecure

_____I have to cope with guilt

_____I want help to be more spontaneous

_____I look forward to the opportunities

Other_____

Discuss your responses and ways to increase one's confidence and effectiveness when sharing the good news.

To Discover Freedom

Some of the best moments in life come in our homes with family and friends. They happen without a printed agenda, over a third cup of coffee, with your feet stretched across the sofa.

During one of those quality times, a friend and fellow follower of Jesus struck with a heavy and startling question. He was thinking about the people who live next door to him and with a troubled tone in his voice mused: *"Why do my neighbors need God?* Joe has a secure job. He recently got an impressive promotion. Their marriage appears to be healthy. Their kids don't give them unusual trouble. They own their house. They buy what they want. They travel more than we do. They seem to have it made. Outside of heaven—*what* does God have to offer to them?"

After an extended and awkward space of silence, the question came in return: *"What do you understand the gospel to be?"*

Jesus responds directly to the issues of *"why"* and *"what"* with the announcement that he had been sent to planet earth *"to proclaim release to the captives"* and *"to set at liberty those who are oppressed"* (Luke 4: 18, rsv).

Our understanding of the gospel is enhanced when we realize that God is not only a "soul-cure" specialist, but he is the one who can rescue the whole person. To make salvation less than a whole-person rescue is to reduce the gospel and restrict the activity of God. Jesus has clarified his own mission at this point and set the ground rules for his disciples who will follow his pattern in history. And now in the Twentieth Century, the shared mission continues to be helping people break out of the prisons they build for themselves.

Jesus knew that all prisons do not have iron bars. He was aware that people build their own padded cells, lock themselves in, and throw away the key. Jesus continues to understand that our external human addictions become forms of captivity. He knows that our internal drives and struggles sap our strength and force us to bow in submission to their power. And still he whispers: "I want to free you from the forces that control you. I want to rescue you from the forms of oppression that inhibit and destroy you."

1. Consider some of those addictions and forces that attack and enslave us. The following lists of "External Forms of Captivity" and "Internal Forms of Oppression" obviously overlap and in some cases belong in both categories. *Accept* this complication. *Study* the suggestions. And *make additions* that are important to you.

EXTERNAL FORMS OF CAPTIVITY	INTERNAL FORMS OF OPPRESSION
Money and Materialism	Egotism
Personal Achievement	Selfishness
Peer Group Approval	Resentment
Marriage—Before or After	Guilt
Pursuit of Education	Greed
Physical Appearances	Lust
Role Playing	Inferiority
Status Seeking	Depression
Desiring Power	Despair
Pursuing Pleasure	Loneliness
New Experiences	Hopelessness
Sexual Behavior	Past Trauma
Pornography	Forms of Fear
Gambling	Pride
Advertising	Worry
Jobs	Anxiety
Organizations	Unforgiveness
Social Pressure	Meaninglessness
Success	Negativism
Alcoholism	Skepticism
Drug Dependencies	Bitterness
Security	Hostility
Occult Forces	Insecurity
Gossip	Self-sufficiency
Sin	Sin

2. Looking at both categories, which forces do you think are most prevalent in your neighborhood, apartment block, on your campus, or in your work world?

3. Identify five of the forces from each list that have exerted their power on you in the past. Discuss some of the ways their controlling power has been subdued.

4. Select at least two areas where you would like to invite God's assistance to help you overcome, and keep in control.

5. In what ways can we help each other escape the overwhelming influence of these forces?

6. Reflect on the teaching in Luke 4: 18. Now answer the questions:

What do I understand the gospel to be?

Why do I need God?

Why do my neighbors need God?

NOTE: The above interpretation and application does not exclude Christian responsibility and participation in restoring justice in our world—"to set at liberty" those peoples who are socially, economically, and politically oppressed.

To Demonstrate the Truth

Robert was a graduate philosophy student. His mind generated honest questions and pushed for reasonable answers. Our paths crossed during a weekend retreat. Our table talk during meals was heavy stuff. Questions that defy complete answers were repeatedly on the menu:

What is your basis for believing God exists?

How can the Scriptures be trusted?

Why does your loving God permit suffering?

What makes your experience more valid than mine?

The discussions were more than game playing. Robert's search was real. We sensed acceptance and understanding of each other. Just before the weekend came in for a landing, we shared one last conversation. Walking in quiet darkness, I linked my arm through his and said, "Friend, in your search, may you find . . . " and while I hesitated with the desire to choose the right words, Robert responded: "May I find the truth."

My reaction was instant and shattered the quietness around us, "That's it—may you find the truth!"

When Jesus announced that part of his mission was to include the *"recovering of sight to the blind,"* beyond the few occasions when he restored physical eyesight to the blind, surely his aim was to correct distorted vision about God's truth. How desperately planet earth needs to hear and see the many facets of God's truth. Our broken and wandering world needs to know:

That truth does exist,

That selfishness is destructive,

That forgiveness is available, and

That God's ways are good and right for all people.

If Jesus committed himself to restore 20/20 vision regarding God's ways, the Christian mission is the same. Followers of Jesus are to use their lips and their living to chase away human blindness and restore sight to eyes that do not recognize the truth.

One dimension of truth that Christians must declare and demonstrate is that *Greatness is found in being a servant.* Jesus modeled his message for a distinct purpose and we see him in action with his disciples in the upper room. (Background Reading: John 13: 1–11.)

John 13: 12–17 (RSV)

> When he had washed their feet, and taken his garments, and resumed his place, he said to them, "Do you know what I have done to you? [13] You call me Teacher and Lord; and you are right, for so I am. [14] If I then, your Lord and Teacher, have washed your feet, you also ought to wash one another's feet. [15] For I have given you an example, that you also should do as I have done to you. [16] Truly, truly, I say to you, a servant is not greater than his master; nor is he who is sent greater than he who sent him. [17] If you know these things, blessed are you if you do them."

1. In secular terms, what are components of *greatness* acknowledged by today's world?

By contrast, what images and thoughts come into your mind when you hear the word *servant?*

_____

_____

_____

_____

_____

_____

_____

_____

_____

_____

2. What principle of leadership does Jesus announce and demonstrate in John 13: 12–17? In a related passage in Mark 10: 42–45, how does Jesus define *greatness*?

3. If you had been in the upper room and experienced Jesus washing your feet—how would you have responded to his question: "Do you know what I have done to you?"

4. In John 13: 17, Jesus distinguishes between *knowing* and *doing*. What is the relationship between the two, and what are the results of doing?

5. What specific instructions does Jesus give his disciples in John 13: 12–17?

6. Washing feet in the manner displayed by Jesus in the upper room was both a cultural and common practice in early New Testament history. Wearing sandals meant your feet got dusty and dirty. Jesus' action was forcefully demonstrating that a servant *perceives* and *responds* to the needs of others. In a contemporary sense—how can we wash each others' feet?

7. Repeat the phrase, "I am a servant," three times.
   What is your private emotional response?

Is the idea distasteful to you?

Does the role attract and appeal to you?

Are you comfortable with a servant identity?

The marks of a servant include his refusal to be preoccupied with his own needs to the exclusion of the needs of others. The servant is more concerned about serving than being served.

8. Think about acts of footwashing—deeds of thoughtfulness and care you can give away to the people in your life. Make additions to the following list. Write the names of at least five different people beside the suggestions listed below.

_____ an unexpected gift
_____ listening ears and eyes
_____ a letter or card
_____ a telephone call
_____ a single rose
_____ a drop-in visit
_____ an "I love you"
_____ a second chance
_____ a word of encouragement
_____ forgiveness
_____ a check or money order
_____ a genuine compliment
_____ a backrub or neck massage
_____ a clean bathroom
_____ babysit for a weekend
_____ offer to tutor a struggling classmate

9. Reread and reflect on John 13: 17.

7. The Bible Meets You Where You Are
Relating to Your World . . .

Involvement in Your World

Christian Thinking in Your World (I)

Christian Thinking in Your World (II)

Distinctive Living in Your World

Influencing Your World

Involvement in Your World

Satan has pulled a con job on God's people. He has convinced too many followers of Jesus that they are to escape involvement in the world and call it righteousness. He has blurred the distinction between "selective separation" and "simple isolation" from the world, and encouraged God's people to abandon their responsibility to society.

John, chapter 17, clarifies the Christian's relationship with his society. In the setting of the passage—today is Thursday. Tomorrow, Jesus will struggle with the cross and die. In his last hours, Jesus serves as a priest. He represents God to his followers and pleads on their behalf to his Father in heaven.

Jesus used the occasion to leave those important last minute instructions. The situation was serious and there was no time for chitchat. Jesus' mind focused on the big issues. There was an urgent tone in his voice. His prayer dealt with critical concerns. The training period was over. The marching orders for the future were definitive and specific.

John 17: 1–19 (rsv)

When Jesus had spoken these words, he lifted up his eyes to heaven and said, "Father, the hour has come; glorify thy Son that the Son may glorify thee, ² since thou hast given him power over all flesh, to give eternal life to all whom thou hast given him. ³ And this is eternal life, that they know thee the only true God, and Jesus Christ whom thou hast sent. ⁴ I glorified thee on earth, having accomplished the work which thou gavest me to do; ⁵ and now, Father, glorify thou me in thy own presence with the glory which I had with thee before the world was made.

⁶ "I have manifested thy name to the men whom thou gavest me out of the world; thine they were, and thou gavest them to me, and they have kept thy word. ⁷ Now they know that everything that thou hast given me is from thee; ⁸ for I have given them the words which thou gavest me, and they have received them and know in truth that I came from thee; and they have believed that thou didst send me. ⁹ I am praying for them; I am not praying for the world but for those whom thou hast given me, for they are thine; ¹⁰ all mine are thine, and thine are mine, and I am glorified in them. ¹¹ And now I am no more in the world, but they are in the world, and I am coming to thee. Holy Father, keep them in thy name, which thou hast given me, that they may be one, even as we are one. ¹² While I was with them, I kept them in thy name, which thou hast given me; I have guarded them, and none of them is lost but the son of perdition, that the scripture might be fulfilled. ¹³ But now I am coming to thee; and these things I speak in the world, that they may have my joy fulfilled in themselves. ¹⁴ I have given them thy word; and the world has hated them because they are not of the world, even as I am not of the world. ¹⁵ I do not pray that thou shouldst take them out of the world, but that thou shouldst keep them from the evil one. ¹⁶ They are not of the world, even as I am not of the world. ¹⁷ Sanctify them in the truth; thy word is truth. ¹⁸ As thou didst send me into the world, so I have sent them into the world. ¹⁹ And for their sake I consecrate myself, that they also may be consecrated in truth."

1. The passage contains five positive and distinct statements regarding the Christian's relationship to the world. Isolate and identify the statements. (Note: verse 6 and verses 14–18.)

1.

2.

3.

4.

5.

Jesus' teaching sounds like a scrambled puzzle. As soon as a person comes "out of the world," he is "sent into the world," where he is "hated by the world," because he is "not of the world," but he is to stay "in the world."

2. Knowing that God's strategy is to communicate his presence and his ways through his followers to all sectors of society, what does it mean to be "in the world"?

Relate being "in the world" to your major involvements this week and where you will spend your time.

3. Keying on the concept that God's people are to be distinctive, different, and identifiable in the world, what does it mean to be "not of the world"?

How are followers of Jesus to be distinctive?

4. Jesus knows that being involved in the world can be dangerous. In verse 12, he mentions that he had "guarded" his disciples, and in verse 15, Jesus prays that his followers would be "kept from the evil one." How does God guard and protect his people from spiritual disaster while they are in the world?

5. What are some of the "hate" responses that come from the world toward Christian believers?

If you are a Christian, and have not been experiencing any adverse reactions from people, what may you conclude?

_____ My society is extremely apathetic.

_____ Jesus was wrong about how the world reacts.

_____ Times have changed since Jesus was around.

_____ I have been hiding my Christian identity.

_____ I have been content to avoid controversial issues.

_____ I have been unfaithful to my Christian mission.

Other __

6. Referring to his first disciples, Jesus prayed to his Father, "As thou didst send me into the world, so have I sent them into the world." Jesus continues to tell his followers, "Where I have been, I want you to go! What I have done, I want you to do!" Why does God send his people into the world?

7. The puzzle is together. Withdrawal from the world is out. Isolation from one's society is not an option. Accommodation to the world is unacceptable. The mandate is clear. The followers of Jesus are sent to be involved in their world. They are to be participants in their communities. They are to be distinctive in the life of their society.

How do you feel about representing God in your world?

Christian Thinking in Your World (I)

Christian thinking is a lost art in our society. The secular squeeze has left many of God's people gasping for their spiritual lives. Our scientific orientation has spread the rumor that to take God seriously is to commit intellectual suicide. Experience centered Christians have fostered the illusion that God's commandments include, "Thou shalt not think."

The Scriptures are light in the despairing darkness. God still invites both the dull and the brilliant to love him with their minds (Mark 12: 30). Biblical teaching reassures those who follow Jesus that they have within them the mind of Christ (1 Cor. 2: 16). God's invitation is to take a deep mental breath, activate your brain cells, keep your mind awake, and think as Christ thought.

Harry Blamires has written a profound book entitled, *The Christian Mind.* The strength of the book revolves around the following understanding:

> *The Christian mind is built on an informed awareness of what the Christian believes.* Consequently, one is able to filter and measure data and input within that Christian frame of reference.
>
> Whether the data is political or economic, controversial or status quo material, *The equipped Christian mind leads to clear Christian thinking.*
>
> *Christian thinking,* regardless of the subject matter, *is the prerequisite to appropriate Christian action.*

In other words, the development of a Christian mind results in distinctive thinking, that can lead to consistent Christian action. One of the results will be to read the newspaper with the same monitoring system as you study the Scriptures.

SCRIPTURAL REFERENCE POINTS

Isaiah 55: 8–9 (RSV)

For my thoughts are not your thoughts, neither are your ways my ways, says the Lord. For as the heavens are higher than the earth, so are my ways higher than your ways and my thoughts than your thoughts.

1. The biblical statement claims that the Creator is different from his creation—he thinks differently and acts differently than people in our world. Observe society around you, think about your own experience, and discuss the claim.

2. List examples that contrast God's ways and mindset with people's ways of thinking and acting.

GOD'S MINDSET	PEOPLE'S MINDSET

Romans 12: 2 (RSV)

Do not be conformed to this world but be transformed by the renewal of your mind, that you may prove what is the will of God, what is good and acceptable and perfect.

1. Paraphrase (state in your own words) the verse and share your expression.

2. Discuss the meaning of the verse noting what one is warned to avoid, how one is transformed or changed, and the consequences of a renewed mind.

Colossians 2: 8 (RSV)

See to it that no one makes a prey of you by philosophy and empty deceit, according to human tradition, according to the elemental spirits of the universe, and not according to Christ.

1. Paraphrase the verse and share your expression.

2. Discuss the meaning of the verse, giving attention to some of the ideas and understandings about life that you are invited to believe that are in conflict with the teachings of Christ.

The pressure to conform to society's norms continually coerces the serious follower of Jesus. The secular squeeze is applied every day. Without a built-in warning system, the Christian believer will be seduced by the appeal of the world's ways. From the list of secular pressure points identified by the expressions below, check those which wield the most influence over you.

_____ 1. "I'll do it my way"—Be your own authority.

_____ 2. "Keep up with the Joneses"—Money will deliver the good life.

_____ 3. "All is relative"—There is no real right or wrong.

_____ 4. "Get all you can"—Greed is acceptable.

_____ 5. "Eat, drink, and be merry"—Pleasure is the trip to take.

_____ 6. "Fit in; don't make waves"—Approval from others at any cost.

_____ 7. "I'm strong and invincible"—A declaration of independence.

_____ 8. "Science has the answer"—Trust technology to come through.

_____ 9. "Look out for number one"—Selfishness is legitimate.

_____10. "God is a crutch"—Christianity is for weaklings.

PRAY for the mind of Christ so you can think and act as a Christian, and for the resources of God to resist the pressures from the world.

Christian Thinking in Your World (II)

God knows that the Christian who lives in the non-Christian world faces the danger of being seduced by society. In response, part of the equipment for survival that God offers the "new creation in Christ" (2 Cor. 5: 17) is a renewed mind. This reprogramming of our thinking, this renovation of our minds assists our living in the world without conforming to the world's norms. God's people whose minds are awake and aware will face issues distinguishing between what is clearly Christian and what is subtly secular.

The experience of Samuel provides an example for us. (Background Reading: 1 Sam. 16: 1–5 and 8–13.)

1 Samuel 16: 6–7 (RSV)

When they came, he looked on Eliab and thought, "Surely the Lord's anointed is before him" [7] But the Lord said to Samuel, "Do not look on his appearance or on the height of his stature, because I have rejected him; for the Lord sees not as man sees; man looks on the outward appearance, but the Lord looks on the heart."

Samuel had been sent by God to Jesse's family in Bethlehem to select a new king. Samuel acted faithfully and obediently in most ways but missed the mind of God on one crucial matter.

1. Based on the Lord's response to Samuel, what measurements did Samuel use to base his judgment of Eliab's suitability to be king?

If you were to look for a king, what criteria would you establish in your selection process?

2. What alternative criteria to Samuel's does the Lord offer for evaluating people?

What internal or "heart" qualities should we look for in people?

3. Think about some current billboards and TV ads. Analyze some of the advertisements in a couple of secular magazines. What is the basis of their appeal?

4. How are we influenced by the values and mindsets of ad men and fashion designers?

How are we prone to measure people's worth and value?

Is there an unconscious caste system in your thinking?

5. What would be the consequences of our becoming less concerned about people's physical attractiveness, sex appeal, position in society, and personality styles?

6. What can we learn from Samuel's experience regarding our view of people?

How can we help each other continue to focus with God's eyesight?

7. How will Christian thinking regarding how we are to view people affect our interpersonal relationships?

8. The situation calling for Christian mind responses are numerous. Select one example from each of the following lists and offer a response that reflects clear Christian thinking. Add other expressions and issues to the list.

EXPRESSIONS	ISSUES
Bigger is better	Marriage
Do your own thing	Success
If it works, do it	Sexual Behavior
If it feels good, do it	De-personalization
Small is beautiful	Abortion
Take care of yourself first	Television
Love your enemies	Leisure
Clothes make the man	Death
I'll get you for that	Genetic Engineering
Diamonds are a girl's best friend	Economic Disparity

Distinctive Living in Your World

Stag parties are those gala events that are held in honor of a friend who is about to get married. Those celebrations have left their marks on the memories of many minds. A while ago I went to one of those events and came home stunned—not stoned—just stunned!

My condition was caused because this particular stag party was unusual. There was no booze and getting bombed. There was no damaging the dignity of sex. Instead, there was a group of guys eating and indulging in significant conversation, singing and finding reasons to laugh, praying and celebrating the Lord's Supper, and sharing their hopes for tomorrow's groom. You see, the event was a Christian stag party. The people present were all followers of Jesus . . . and that made a difference because followers of Jesus are different!

A common Christian strategy for being different in society has been to avoid "worldliness." The Scriptures have provided the incentive to escape worldliness by exclaiming, "To be a friend of the world is to be an enemy of God" (James 4: 4). The difficulty confronting God's people has been to arrive at a common understanding about what is "worldly" without developing a negative and distorted reputation about what is "Christian."

Discuss the following definition of "worldliness." List a few examples that contrast society's values with God's ideals.

> WORLDLINESS is embracing the values, attitudes, and behavior approved by our society—as our own—when they stand in conflict with God's ideals for his people.

SOCIETY'S VALUES	GOD'S VALUES

One crucial area where the Christian must demonstrate a distinctive attitude and value system is in the realm of money. In contrast with North American behavior patterns, Jesus was adamant as he proclaimed, "man shall not live by bread alone"

(Matt. 4: 4), and "man's life does not consist in the abundance of possessions" (Luke 12: 15).

Matthew 6: 19–33 (rsv)

Do not lay up for yourselves treasures on earth, where moth and rust consume and where thieves break in and steal, [20] but lay up for yourselves treasures in heaven, where neither moth nor rust consumes and where thieves do not break in and steal. [21] For where your treasure is, there will your heart be also.

[22] The eye is the lamp of the body. So, if your eye is sound, your whole body will be full of light; [23] But if your eye is not sound, your whole body will be full of darkness. If then the light in you is darkness, how great is the darkness!

[24] No one can serve two masters; for either he will hate the one and love the other, or he will be devoted to the one and despise the other. You cannot serve God and mammon. [25] Therefore I tell you, do not be anxious about your life, what you shall eat or what you shall drink, nor about your body, what you shall put on. Is not life more than food, and the body more than clothing? [26] Look at the birds of the air: they neither sow nor reap nor gather into barns, and yet your heavenly Father feeds them. Are you not of more value than they? [27] And which of you by being anxious can add one cubit to his span of life? [28] And why are you anxious about clothing? Consider the lilies of the field, how they grow; they neither toil nor spin; [29] yet I tell you, even Solomon in all his glory was not arrayed like one of these. [30] But if God so clothes the grass of the field, which today is alive and tomorrow is thrown into the oven, will he not much more clothe you, O men of little faith? [31] Therefore do not be anxious, saying, "What shall we eat?" or "What shall we drink?" or "What shall we wear?" [32] For the Gentiles seek all these things; and your heavenly Father knows that you need them all. [33] But seek first his kingdom and his righteousness, and all these things shall be yours as well.

ANALYZING THE PASSAGE

1. Verses 19–21: Where does Jesus instruct his followers to invest their resources?

Where does Jesus say your predominate interest will be?

2. Verses 22–23: What will be the result of good eyesight or a clear view of reality?

3. Verse 24: Why is it impossible to serve two gods at the same time?

4. Verses 25–32: What aspects of life does Jesus instruct his people to stop worrying about?

What reasons are offered why one should stop being over-anxious?

5. Verse 33: From the context of the passage, in return for giving your top priority to God and his kingdom, what things shall be yours as well?

APPLYING THE PASSAGE

1. How does one invest in eternal "treasures in heaven"?

How does one invest in temporal "treasures on earth"?

2. God promises that if we serve him first, he will take care of our needs. Why is so much of our wishing, thinking, and acting time spent on our self-centered desires rather than on God's goals and the needs of others?

3. Observation and personal experience tells us that many of Jesus' followers often want the best of both worlds. They announce with their lifestyles that they want all the material goodies and experiences secular society can serve on its silver platter. Plus they want Jesus and his benefits as a bonus. Do you think a person can have the best of both worlds? Why? Why not?

PERSONALIZING THE PASSAGE

1. Are you attracted by the money madness mentality of our age? Do you believe the secular fomula: "More money + additional things = the good life"?

2. Where do you invest your money?

How much money do you keep for your own needs and desires?

How much money do you invest in "stuff" that eventually ends up in the garbage dump?

How much money do you invest in the interests of the Kingdom of God?

How much do you give to worthy Kingdom organizations?

How much do you give to people in need without feeling the necessity of an income tax receipt?

3. How much of your creativity and dream time is focused on:

Devising schemes to invest yourself and your money more effectively in God's work and other people's needs?

Calculating ways to acquire more "stuff" and pile up the perishable?

4. Money is a dangerous commodity. Jesus said it would be tough for the rich to get into the Kingdom of Heaven. In this particular passage, Jesus insists that you cannot serve God and money at the same time.

How important is money and its benefits to you? Is your decision making controlled by financial consideration?

Are you in control or are you being controlled by the power of money?

If you are a Christian, is your attitude and behavior regarding money different from that of your non-Christian neighbor or friend?

5. When you hear Jesus saying: "Seek first the kingdom of God and his righteousness," what issues of response and obedience does that principle raise for you?

Influencing Your World

Thermometers and thermostats are a couple of technology's better ideas.

Thermometers serve the useful purpose of recording our temperatures. Like the hands of a watch announce the time, thermometers register temperatures but in no way regulate them.

Thermostats serve a different and more noble purpose. They regulate and control the temperature. Like a water pressure valve that permits only a certain amount of water to flow through a hose, a thermostat determines how much heat flows out of a furnace.

Christians are meant to be thermostats in their world! Unfortunately, God's people are too often thermometers. Instead of influencing and affecting their world around them, many Christians simply reflect the norms of their society.

In the sermon on the Mount, Jesus used two metaphors to delineate a strategy for being a thermostat and influencing one's world. He said his followers were "the salt of the earth" and "the light of the world." Notice that Jesus did not instruct his people to be "the sugar of their society"!

Matthew 5: 13 (RSV)

You are the salt of the earth; but if salt has lost its taste, how shall its saltness be restored? It is no longer good for anything except to be thrown out and trodden under foot by men.

Matthew 5: 14–16 (RSV)

You are the light of the world. A city set on a hill cannot be hid. [15] Nor do men light a lamp and put it under a bushel, but on a stand, and it gives light to all in the house. [16] Let your light so shine before men, that they may see your good works and give glory to your Father who is in heaven.

1. Where are God's people to be salt? What assessment does Jesus make of salt that has lost its savor?

2. Before the time when refrigerators were common, salt was used as an effective preservative. For example, salt sprinkled on fresh beef would preserve that meat and prevent the process of decay.
Name five values and virtues that you think God would like to preserve in our world.

     1.

     2.

     3.

     4.

     5.

Does the role of preventing decay in society make the Christian a moral minus sign—always negative? Why or why not?

3. Food without salt is often flat and bland. The right amount of salt brings out the rich flavor in food. Too much salt is offensive to our taste. When are Christians:
Not salty enough?

Too salty?

Being the right amount of salt?

4. Some churches may be serving as salt shakers that never get turned upside down. All the salt gets collected together and stays as a clump inside the shaker. If Jesus were on earth again and speaking to a church like that on a Sunday morning, what do you think he would say?

5. Change your focus to the "light" metaphor. Where are God's people to be light?
a.

b.

How are Christians to be light in the world (Matt. 5: 14–16)?

What effect does light have on darkness?

Which is stronger—light or darkness?

What should Christian light reveal?

Eliminating the bright, public lights—the extraordinary 1000 watt light bulbs—who are some of God's lights that you admire and respect? Why do you respect them?

6. In what ways does God want you to be "salt" and "light"?

When Jesus was on planet earth, he claimed, "I am the light of the world" (John 9: 5). In his absence, Jesus has decreed that his followers are the "light of the world." When Jesus was present in human form, he sprinkled salt on his culture and influenced his society. Now, in relationship with that same Jesus, God's people can influence their world for good and right.

PRAYER: Father, we confess that rather than influencing our world, we are often influenced by our world. Forgive us. May we know You, so we can "walk as children of light."

Bible Study Helps

Guides for Small Group Leaders

Guides for Small Group Members

Guides for Small Group Leaders

1. PRE-STUDY AND PREPARATION IS A MUST

Spend time with the passage to be studied even though you may be following a prepared outline. Pray. Let the Spirit lead you both before and during the study.

2. DON'T DOMINATE YOUR GROUP SESSION

You have not been given a personal pulpit to parade your wisdom. Resist the temptation to be an authority on every issue. Relax and be the real you. Give others the chance to be themselves too.

3. DON'T ABDICATE YOUR LEADERSHIP ROLE

Control the direction of the discussion. Allow detours when the subject has value but keep the primary focus on the Scriptures and content of the study.

4. ENCOURAGE PARTICIPATION FROM ALL GROUP MEMBERS

Develop ways of controlling the extrovert and building confidence in the introvert. Like, "Can we hear some ideas from those who have not expressed themselves yet?" or, "George, what is your reaction?"

5. LEARN HOW TO TAKE PEOPLE OFF THE HOOK GRACIOUSLY WHEN
   THEY MAKE "OUT OF IT" COMMENTS

Like, "Thank you for those comments; are there other ideas?" or, pick out one thought or phrase from the ramblings that does apply and comment, "What I hear you saying is. . . . Does someone else have a point to bring up?"

6. PREDETERMINE NEVER TO EMBARRASS ANYONE

Learn the art of taking issue with people who are off the biblical target without putting them down personally. Affirm the truth without belittling personalities.

7. BE ALERT FOR NON VERBAL COMMUNICATION

Take note of moist eyes, harsh tone quality, quivering voice patterns, the withdrawn indication to speak, raised eyebrows, the dropped head, etc. Then respond appropriately to what you have observed. No response may be the right response.

8. VARY THE FORMAT AND UTILIZE DIFFERENT METHODS

Let your creativity generate surprises for your group members. Be unpredictable regarding the form the sessions will take. Have a game plan but be ready to change your strategy.

9. ASK OPEN-ENDED, PURSUING, AND CLARIFYING QUESTIONS

Ask questions that cannot be answered with a direct "yes" or "no." Like, "What do you think Jesus meant when he said . . ." or "If what you say is true, then . . ." or "Give us an example of what you mean."

10. PUSH THE GROUP'S CONCLUSIONS TO THEIR LOGICAL APPLICA-
      TIONS FOR NOW

Bible study must result in action or the purpose is incomplete. Accelerate that process by consistently asking, "How does what we are saying apply to our daily living?"

11. MAKE SUMMARY STATEMENTS AT THE END OF YOUR SESSION

Tie the discussion down with capsule comments that summarize the main points derived from the study.

12. BE READY TO SHARE AND RELINQUISH YOUR LEADERSHIP

Ask yourself, "Who else can lead this group?" and give others the opportunity to develop their skills.

Guides for Small Group Members

1. EXPECT TO LEARN FROM EACH OTHER
Have confidence in the insight and experience of your fellow group members. Let them teach you.

2. CREATE AN ATMOSPHERE FOR FREEDOM OF EXPRESSION
Be setting-conscious. Be sure the group members can see and hear each other. Get rid of excess noise and other forms of distraction. Be honest yourself and expect honesty from others.

3. MAINTAIN THE FREEDOM TO DISAGREE WITH EACH OTHER
Realize that it is not necessary to agree with each other to be united and care about each other. Affirm rather than judge. Don't expect conformity. Avoid stereotyping.

4. TAKE EACH OTHER'S OPINIONS AND PERSPECTIVES SERIOUSLY
Each group member will be in different space mentally and spiritually. Be sensitive to where people are in their process of becoming. Do nothing to depreciate anyone's worth or importance.

5. DEVELOP AN AWARENESS AND SENSITIVITY TOWARD EACH OTHER
Foster a genuine interest in what is happening in each other's lives. Ask yourself, "Who in the group is hurting, facing special stress, or giving us a reason to celebrate."

6. COMMIT YOURSELF TO THE DEVELOPMENT OF QUALITY RELATIONSHIPS
Relationships that matter are costly involvements. Failure to pay the price of involvement with people leads to personal poverty.

7. BE CAREFUL NOT TO ALIENATE ANYONE FROM THE GROUP
Appreciate and respect diversity. Let an attitude of acceptance make the non-Christian feel at ease. Avoid cliches and "Christianese" communication.

8. DON'T BE AFRAID OF SILENCE
"The sound of silence" helps people think and reflect on the teach-

ing of the passage. Don't interrupt the ministry of the Holy Spirit with useless chatter.

9. IN THE SMALL GROUP BIGGER IS NOT BETTER

A group of eight is ideal. When the number of people in the group reaches twelve, splitting into two groups should be considered.

10. MINISTER TO EACH OTHER

Be prepared to give and receive. Don't short-circuit God's strategy for his people to minister and care for each other.

11. REALIZE THAT SOME SESSIONS WILL BE MORE EFFECTIVE THAN OTHERS

Avoid depression when your expectations for a session are not met. Trust God to do his work through the power of his Word. Place your confidence in the aliveness of the Holy Spirit.

12. DON'T CONFINE YOUR RELATIONSHIPS TO THE TIMES YOUR GROUP GETS TOGETHER

The thoughtful phone call, a note expressing care and concern, an invitation into your home and life will deepen relationships and make the group experience more valuable.